D0214367

Library of Congress Subject Headings: Philosophy, Practice, and Prospects

ABOUT THE AUTHOR

William E. Studwell, MSLS, is Principal Cataloger and Associate Professor, University Libraries, Northern Illinois University in DeKalb. He has written many articles for some of the leading library and information science journals, including over two dozen articles on subject cataloging. His other publications include several reference books and a forthcoming workbook on cataloging books. He received his master's degree from Catholic University in Washington DC.

Library of Congress Subject Headings: Philosophy, Practice, and Prospects

William E. Studwell

The Haworth Press
New York • London

Library of Congress Subject Headings: Philosophy, Practice, and Prospects is Volume Number 2 in the Haworth Series in Cataloging & Classification.

The Haworth Press, Inc., 10 Alice Street, Binghamton, NY 13904-1580
EUROSPAN/Haworth, 3 Henrietta Street, London WC2E 8LU England

Library of Congress Cataloging-in-Publication Data

Studwell, William E. (William Emmett), 1936-
Library of Congress subject headings : philosophy, practice, and prospects / William E. Studwell.
p. cm.
Includes bibliographical references.
ISBN 1-56024-003-2
1. Subject headings, Library of Congress – Evaluation. 2. Subject cataloging – Philosophy. 3. Subject cataloging. I. Title.
Z695.Z8L527 1990
025.4'9 – dc20

89-26970
CIP

CONTENTS

ALL HAWORTH BOOKS & JOURNALS
ARE PRINTED ON CERTIFIED
ACID-FREE PAPER

Preface

The quest for principles, foundations, and theories is one of the noblest human intellectual endeavours. Through the ages man has sought to understand natural and cultural phenomena in order to make sense out of life and its riches. On one hand, scientific inquiry has set itself to investigate and subsequently explain nature. On the other hand, cultural artifacts have been predicated on philosophical, sociological, anthropological or linguistical analysis.

Among the contemporary cultural artifacts, *Library of Congress Subject Headings* system stands out as a monumental encyclopedia of knowledge in the form of a controlled vocabulary. For almost three quarters of a century, this encyclopedia has reflected the universe of knowledge based on literary warrant by means of additions and deletions of terms and references. Originally intended as a tool for subject retrieval in the Library of Congress dictionary catalogs, it has evolved through the years into a national and international "standard" and is used by catalogers in almost all English speaking countries. In fact, English Canadian academic and research libraries have followed for the most part of this century L.C. cataloguing practice and hence have used North American tools for the construction of their catalogues. Furthermore, *Library of Congress Subject Headings* have been supplemented by *Canadian Subject Headings*[1] so as to reflect historical and political patterns unique to Canada.

In order to achieve national cataloguing consistency, French Canadian libraries have also followed closely L.C. practice, in French! Cataloguing tools such as AACR1, AACR2, and the recent AACR2 1/2 have been translated into French. Since 1962, librarians at Université Laval (Québec city) have translated L.C.S.H. into French published under the title *Répertoire de vedettes-matière*.[2] Since then, the National Library of Canada, the Bibliothèque nationale du Québec and the Université de Montréal have joined together to expand and update the list. The *Répertoire* is used, with adaptations, by the Bibliothèque nationale in Paris and serves as a basis for the trilingual (English, Dutch, French) thesaurus of the Bibliothèque royale de Belgique. It has become a "standard" for the French speaking cataloguing community. L.C.S.H. is consequently a system that reaches far beyond the United States. Its impact on subject cataloguing and retrieval cannot be overly stressed.

William Studwell is no newcomer on the subject cataloguing scene: twenty five years of daily practical experience and author, in the last decade, of close to twenty five articles on suggestions for improvement of the L.C.S.H. system. The depth of his knowledge of the system and his critical appraisals of it prove beyond doubt that he is one of a rare species: a scholar cataloger. His seminal article "Why not an 'AACR' for Subject Headings"[3] brought about the meeting of two minds and concerns across an international border, a language distinctiveness and a complementary professional commitment.

Subject cataloguing is an art as Studwell rightly asserts. It lends itself to the cataloger's subjectivity and, in reverse pattern, to the catalogue user's subjectivity. Not that subjectivity is "wrong" per se; it does manifest the human touch, creativity, and bias. For lack of sound theoretical basis and principles in the creation and applications of L.C.S.H. "fuzziness between the role of the L.C. subject heading system and the role of the application of L.C. subject headings" has crept over the years in subject catalogues. Will anarchy replace fuzziness in the twenty-first century?

To partly obviate this problem, quality graduate education and training is mandatory. Julia Pettee's despair is still very much with us: "Subject headings . . . Frankly we don't know how to teach them."[4] We have been struggling in trying to teach the "how" of subject headings but the "why" remains elusive for lack of clear, systematic, universal stated principles for the creation and application of subject headings in any language. It is hoped that this book will contribute to the creation of a code for subject cataloguing strongly called for by practitioners and teachers alike.

Paule Rolland-Thomas
Professor
Ecole de bibliothéconomie
et des sciences de l'information
Université de Montréal
Montréal (Canada)

REFERENCES

1. *Canadian Subject Headings*. 2nd ed. Ottawa: National Library of Canada, 1985.

2. *Répertoire de vedettes-matière*. 9e éd. Québec: Bibliothèque de l'Université Laval, 1983.

3. William E. Studwell, "Why not an 'AACR' for Subject Headings?," *Cataloging & Classification Quarterly* 6, no. 1: 3-9 (Fall 1985).

4. Julia Peettee, *Subject Headings: The History and Theory of the Alphabetical Subject Approach to Books*. New York: H.W. Wilson, 1946, p. 4.

Introduction

Whether one calls it subject cataloging, subject retrieval, subject access, subject analysis, subject heading work, or a similar term, the word "subject" is always the key concept. That is, an intellectual process is being performed to determine the topic(s) or contents of an item, and to express the topic(s) or contents in structure and terminology which is readily understood by and mutually-acceptable to both the producer (the cataloger) and the consumer (the library user). When any part of this process is faulty, the capability for locating the material desired is thereby potentially reduced. If the subject cataloging system itself is deficient, a problem exists. If the interpretation of the subject cataloging system by the cataloger is deficient, another problem exists. Or if either the system or its everyday practical manifestation in subject headings are imperfectly interfaced by the library user, yet another problem exists.

There have been many deficiencies in all three of these components of subject retrieval over the years, and yet the process has functioned reasonably well. But it is capable of performing better, and as time goes on the process may be faced with even greater demands in light of the increasing volume of material to be accessed, the higher complexity of online bibliographic catalogs, and the potentially greater expectations and diminished patience of the library user. This volume is an effort to contribute towards the improvement of the theoretical bases of subject cataloging, specifically the subject heading system established by the Library of Congress. The first two of the above-mentioned three components of effective subject access, the system of subject cataloging and its interpretation, will be covered in considerable detail. The third component, the user's contact with subject access, will be touched upon to some extent, but much of this component falls under the umbrella of reference service, user education, and bibliographic instruction and thereby does not directly involve the subject cataloging process.

The ideas presented in this book are entirely personal, based upon the perceptions gained by about twenty-five years of everyday practical cataloging or indexing work and the knowledge acquired by theoretical research for about twenty-five articles on subject cataloging. All of the material except quoted passages is this author's opinion or observations, although some of it may coincide with ideas previously put into print or expressed in some other way. Only theoretical, conceptual, and philosophical matters, along with their practical manifestations, are included in this volume. Accordingly, there is little of value for those persons seeking an everyday guide to understanding and using Library of Congress (LC) subject headings. This is solely intended to be a medium for stimulating thought about LC subject headings and expediting possible improvements. In part, LC's current subject heading policies, whether clearly stated or simply implied, are presented in a theoretical context. In part, other ideas and perceptions that are not currently espoused by LC or in fact are in conflict with current LC practice are also presented. Or in other words, this is an amalgamation of the author's view of what is and what should be in the complicated world of LC subject headings. Although a number of criticisms of LC policy and practice are made, this should not be considered as an attack on LC or its subject heading system. It is not intended to tear down LC, but to build it even stronger. As will be evident early in the book, this author has a high regard for the basic characteristics and effectiveness of LC. But that does not mean that changes are not in order.

The ultimate purpose of this book is a collegial attempt to help improve the understandability and clarity of the system, increase consistency and collocation, increase the number of effective access points, facilitate the interface of the system with the computer, and in other ways make the Library of Congress subject heading system and its application of even greater value to the cataloger and the user. Except when necessary, there is no intent to compare LC with other systems. LC and only LC is being considered. The introduction of external elements into the already complex and sometimes confusing LC environment would be, in this author's opinion, of no help at this time. However, as will be shown later, the author definitely does support the introduction of new ideas compatible with the basic LC framework.

The material is presented in three parts. The first section, "The System," deals with the basic philosophical foundations of LC subject headings. Thirty-two "principles" (guidelines, suggestions, or statements) are offered along with detailed explanations, examples, and their relationships to other principles (for example, how inversions and structural inconsistency are related). Since the principles are not given in a vacuum but rather in the practical context of everyday subject cataloging, the principles may touch upon one another and even clearly overlap. The principles are divided into five subcategories: general considerations; structural matters; terminology and language; specificity and detail; and presentation of subject heading data, or communication of subject heading information, in the various printed and online subject cataloging tools issued by LC.

The second section, "Application," deals with matters of subject cataloging practice, or interpretation and application of LC subject headings. Again, principles are offered along with explanations, examples, and their relationships to other principles (for example, how "secondary headings" and order of headings are related). In this second section, there are fifteen principles of similar characteristics, nature and function as in the first section. The principles are divided into five subcategories: general considerations; "secondary headings"; number of subject headings assigned; order of subject headings assigned; and parallelism of subject headings. Altogether, it is felt that the forty-seven principles comprise at least a good start toward solid theoretical framework to guide the Library of Congress subject heading system and its application. Throughout the first two sections, the author's own terminology was employed, along with the necessary definitions. One of the difficulties with LC subject headings is the lack of clear terms for some subject phenomena, and the inadequacy of the terms used by LC for other subject phenomena.

It should be noted that the subject heading examples used were derived from the 11th edition of *Library of Congress Subject Headings* (LCSH). But the use of the 11th edition does not mean that the purpose of this study is an explication or analysis of that particular edition. The ideas presented here are intended to be of wider scope, broader applicability, and longer term value than one specific spot in time and space. Furthermore, since LC is making changes at a rapid pace, it is possible that some of the examples given or problems presented may no longer be valid. To save on the number of footnotes, examples from the 11th edition were not cited.

The third section, "The Future," looks ahead to future issues relating to subject cataloging, such as the development of a theoretical subject heading code, the interface of LC subject headings with the computer, and some speculation as to the role and nature of LC subject headings in the years to come. A bibliography on subject cataloging is given at the end of the book. The bibliography contains citations used in this volume plus other items useful to gain a broader understanding of subject cataloging.

Finally, one general observation about subject cataloging should be made here. While based on standards and printed on online authority tools, cataloging is as least as much an art as it is a science. Such is even more true for subject cataloging, which is to a large extent dependent on the interpretation and communication skills of the subject cataloger. If this fundamental premise is not kept in the forefront of our perceptions of subject access, then a true and realistic view of the process cannot be attained. Improvement of the subject heading system will go a long way to make the work of the artist/subject cataloger easier and more reliable, but even with the best of systems the background and capabilities of the subject cataloger are a key consideration. It is not easy to be a subject cataloger, for the subject of cataloging process requires a substantial amount of knowledge and skill, plus the ability to make confident decisions. This characteristic of subject cataloging has perhaps been a factor in the slowness toward full, consistent, and logical development of Library of Congress subject headings. With an inevitable degree of subjectivity in the subject process, and long-term fuzziness between the role of the LC subject heading system and the role of the application of LC subject headings, the delay in the maturation of the subject access process to the same level as the descriptive cataloging process is quite understandable.

Lately, though, there appears to be an accelerating interest in subject cataloging and its betterment throughout the library community, and LC clearly has made improvements in the structure/logic, terminology/semantics, and detail/specificity of LC subject headings in recent years. So the time to try to develop the subject heading system to its fullest potential is probably at hand. It is hoped that this book, which will no doubt be controversial, will help prepare the way for subject access' entrance into the uncertain requirements of the imminent twenty-first century.

Chapter 1

The System: Philosophy and Problems

The philosophy or theoretical principles of Library of Congress subject headings have never been comprehensively formulated or presented in print by the Library of Congress or by outside persons or organizations. Some theoretical aspects of LC subject headings have appeared in various publications, but such efforts have been scattered and very incomplete. Some specific suggestions to improve LC subject headings have been put forth but these again have been limited. And some overall descriptions of how the LC subject heading system works or is supposed to work have also been brought forth, but these competent publications have primarily focused on exposition of the present system instead of analysis and theory.

To fill this void, thirty-two principles relating to the LC subject heading system are offered below. There is no pretense that these principles, nor the fifteen principles in the section on the application of LC subject headings, in any way comprise all of the possible knowledge in the area. It is hoped, however, that the formulation of these principles will be a substantial first step towards the development of a comprehensive and widely-agreed upon set of principles.

PRINCIPLES RELATING TO THE LIBRARY OF CONGRESS SUBJECT HEADING SYSTEM (STRUCTURE, TERMINOLOGY, DOCUMENTATION, AND OTHER TOPICS)

A. General

1. The Library of Congress subject heading system, though far from perfect, is a work of collective, cumulative, and increasing genius;

it should not be discarded in favor of less-established and unproven alternatives

The Library of Congress subject heading system has been in existence for nearly a century. During that time it has progressed from a small list for use by just the Library of Congress to a huge and complex system which is widely utilized around the English-speaking world and beyond (for example, in France and French Canada). No other system is as pervasive nor as dominant. The system has a large number of major and minor faults, but it would be quite unrealistic to expect perfection from any organism of this size and scope. Even geniuses like Bach, Beethoven, Mozart, and Tchaikovsky did not always produce great works and the human body is a complex marvel of biological genius, yet it is riddled with imperfections. Similarly, the LC subject heading system, with all its flaws, is in this author's opinion, an overall entity of genius. As it continues to mature, the genius of LC's system becomes more and more apparent.[1]

If some persons cannot concede that LC's subject heading system is a work of increasing genius, at least LC's premier international position as a tool for verbal subject access must be admitted. Other systems, such as PRECIS, have been offered as alternatives to LC, but LC should definitely not be discarded for three reasons. First, the other systems really have not proven themselves on a long-term basis and in a wide-scale environment. Second, LC is improving at an accelerating rate. Not every recent change by LC has been for the better, but as a whole there have been many improvements in structure, terminology, and specifity during the past decade or so. A substantial proportion of the improvements, of course, were influenced by the appearance of the computer. And third, the economic, administrative, intellectual, and psychological disadvantages of replacing the widely-used and long-established LC system would be enormous. Since no overwhelming evidence has been presented that any of the other systems would clearly and decidedly be superior, it is preferable to stay with what has worked in the past. Remember what Winston Churchill said about democracy, "No one pretends that democracy is perfect or all-wise. Indeed, it has been said that democracy is the worst form of government except all those other forms that have been tried from time to time."[2] The same applies to the Library of Congress' subject heading system. Although it has many shortcomings, it still is the best comprehensive, all-purpose system we have for verbal subject retrieval.

2. The Library of Congress cannot presume that problems of subject heading application are primarily a matter of the cataloger's experience, knowledge, and ability; LC must do their best to provide clear and consistent structure, terminology, and presentation of data (i.e., communication of subject heading information), and to provide sufficient detail and specificity for all reasonable needs

Over the years, it has been this author's observation that one of the flaws of the Library of Congress' subject heading system is a subtle yet perceptible tendency by LC to presume that shortcomings in the everyday use of the subject heading system are basically the fault of the subject cataloger whether at LC or elsewhere. (This frame of mind is a natural and understandable condition of a large and complex organization.) It would be of course ridiculous to claim that even the best-trained and most-talented subject catalogers do not make occasional incorrect or questionable subject cataloging decisions. But any deficiencies in the final product of the process, that is, the subject heading(s) made available to the library user, are potentially the shared responsibility of both system and cataloger. Sometimes the system is at fault, sometimes the cataloger, and sometimes both.

In any case, LC must strive to provide the most clearly understood and most usable system they can. And they should do so not only for the benefit of their own catalogers, but for the world as a whole. Whether the Library of Congress likes it or not, their system is very extensively applied by catalogers outside of LC. One of the clearer manifestations of this is the OCLC system which as of June 30, 1988, contained about 12,520,000 non-LC records, or about 70% of its total data base.[3] Not all of these non-LC records used LC subject headings, but certainly a strong majority did. Therefore LC has a degree of obligation to serve the needs of those beyond their walls.[4] The internationally utilized system must have logical and consistent structure and terminology, very clear communication of subject headings and their usage to the subject cataloger and library patron, and adequate detail and specificity. This goal will more easily be achieved if LC approaches the task with the presumption that any aspect of their subject heading system is potentially a problem for the cataloger or library user. Such self-criticism and analysis may go far in making a very good system into a considerably better system.

3. Consistency is the single most important characteristic in subject cataloging

While it is highly desirable that descriptive cataloging and subject cataloging be both clear and consistent, there is some difference of emphasis between descriptive cataloging on one hand and subject cataloging on the other. The most important consideration in descriptive cataloging is that the cataloging data be clearly understood by the library user. Except for name forms, consistency between bibliographical records is not as vital as clarity. In contrast, subject cataloging has to be more concerned with consistency than with absolute understandability or a consensus as to the precise form of headings. For example, whether the term "Biological chemistry" or the term "Biochemistry" is used is less important than the assurance that the concept of this discipline be consistently represented in the subject access system, and that the variant term leads by reference to the official term. Similarly, whether "Brazil--Economic conditions" or "Brazil--Economic conditions--History" is used for the economic history of that country is less important than the assurance that only one form for the concept is permitted by the system. The same situation also applies to "Universities and colleges" versus "Colleges and universities," "West Germany" versus "Germany (West)," "Unesco" versus "United Nations Educational, Scientific and Cultural Organization," and numerous others.

Overall, consistency has to be the prime motivator of LC's subject heading system as well as the prime motivator for the interpretation and application of LC subject headings. Consistency is, along with collocation and understandability, one of the three goals of a subject access system. (These three goals greatly overlap and are somewhat conflicting.) Collocation is a fundamental byproduct of consistency and therefore is subordinate to consistency. And understandability or clarity, which is also considerably influenced by consistency, is, as discussed above, less essential than consistency.

The supreme importance of consistency, furthermore, pertains to all aspects of LC's subject heading system, including structure, terminology, specificity, and presentation of data. If the theme of consistency is not at the forefront of our thinking about subject cataloging, and accordingly consistency is not pervasive or thoroughly evident throughout the subject cataloging process, the effectiveness of subject cataloging is most certainly reduced. In other words, the greater the degree of consistency (or predictability), the greater the effectiveness of subject access.

B. Structure

1. Structural elements in LC subject headings must be simple

"Structural element" is this author's designation for each individual part of an LC subject heading which is separated or potentially separable by a double dash (--). Subject headings without any double dashes contain only one structural element. There are two types of structural elements in LC subject headings, primary or initial structural elements and subordinate structural elements or subdivisions. Some persons may view this terminology as verbose, but the commonly used alternatives "Subject headings" and "Subdivisions" are quite unclear. Subject headings can be only one word or a long string of terms which includes subdivisions. The terminology must clearly separate the two differing functions.

Subordinate structural elements/subdivisions have received much attention from LC and cause relatively few problems. Primary structural elements/initial structural elements, in contrast, are more troublesome. In addition to difficulties that may be caused by questionable terminology or by poor presentation of data to the subject cataloger and library user, making the structure of the primary structural element overly complex risks reduced subject access. As an illustration, "Lawyers" is a one word primary structural element expressing a single concept. When a second word is added to

"Lawyers," creating headings such as "Minority lawyers," "Patent lawyers," or "Women lawyers," the primary structural element becomes more complex by expressing two concepts. A case could be made for handling these dual concept subjects as two separate single concept headings, that is, "Minorities" plus "Lawyers," "Patents" plus "Lawyers," and "Women" plus "Lawyers." But since the three dual concept headings represent naturally occurring and common phenomena, and appear in the literature, the dual concept structure is preferable.

When a complex structure has even the slightest element of artificiality, unnaturalness, or strain to logic or language, however, a simpler structure should be favored. Any three concept headings should especially be seriously questioned, although not necessarily forbidden. Using the examples given above, headings such as "Minority patent lawyers," "Jewish patent lawyers," "Left-handed minority lawyers," "Women patent lawyers," and "Aged women lawyers" should definitely be avoided. Instead, a set of two headings, based on currently available headings, should be used for each of the occasions:

Patent lawyers
Minority lawyers
Patent lawyers
Lawyers, Jewish
Minority lawyers
Left- and right-handedness
Patent lawyers
Women lawyers
Women lawyers
Aged women

Even many two concept headings are questionable, for example, "Left-handed lawyers," "Left-handed women," "Left-handed aged," and "Aged lawyers." If there is any doubt at all about establishing a multiple-concept primary structural element, the simpler structure should prevail. As a whole, LC to their credit has tended to stay with simpler structure headings, with the exception of some inversions and subjects with the compound structures "[topic] and [topic]," "[topic] as [topic]," and "[topic] in [topic]." (Alternatives to these patterns will be offered below in B9.) Multiple-concept subjects have been established by LC with more frequency in recent years, however, and this trend should be viewed with caution. At the same time, they have of late tended to change some types of compound headings into simpler structural forms, for example, "Carbohydrate metabolism disorders" to "Carbohydrates--Metabolism--Disorders."

2. Structural elements in LC subject headings must be consistent

In the above principle, the LC-established subject heading "Lawyers, Jewish" was used in an example. Conceptually, there is nothing wrong with this heading. Structurally, though, there are two problems. First, it is an unnecessary inversion. (Inverted subjects and the difficulties they create will be dealt with shortly.) Second, it is inconsistent in structure with other primary structural elements of similar purpose. "Lawyers, Jewish" and two other headings "Lawyers, Blind" and "Lawyers, Foreign" are structurally at odds with another group of related headings which includes "Minority lawyers," "Women lawyers," and "Afro-American lawyers." There is no valid reason for this structural inconsistency, and all such cases should be rectified thus not only improving structure but positively affecting collocation.

But when the primary structural element contains two concepts, as in all of the above examples, it is vital that the concept which is not the initial term is scrupulously see-referenced (LC has been generally doing this well in recent years). In that way, all multiple-concept primary structural elements can be accessed either as the official heading or via the see-reference mechanism. Accordingly, all multiple-concept primary structural elements containing terms such as "Lawyers," "Jewish," and "Blind" can be gathered together in one way or another. (This necessity for cross-referencing is another reason to prefer simpler primary structural elements.) Other examples of inconsistent primary structural elements established by LC, again using the terms treated above, are "Jewish athletes" versus "Athletes, Blind," "Jewish children" versus "Children, Blind," "Jewish aged" versus "Aged, Blind," and

"Jewish entertainers" versus "Entertainers, Blind." Then within the span of "Jewish" headings there are the inconsistencies "Jewish authors" versus "Musicians, Jewish," "Jewish etiquette" versus "Ethics, Jewish," and "Jewish fiction" versus "Legends, Jewish." All of these inconsistencies can be resolved by the simple technique of eliminating the inversions.

But by no means are all structural inconsistencies in primary structural elements caused by inversions. Once again going into familiar territory, there are the inconsistencies "Blind--Books and reading" versus "Maps for the blind" versus "Blind, Periodicals for the," and the case of military lawyers which is not established by LC as either "Military lawyers" or "Lawyers, Military" but only as a subdivision ("--Lawyers") under particular branches of the armed forces. In the former example, all of the headings should have the same structural patterns, that is, "Blind--Books and reading for," "Blind--Maps for," and "Blind--Periodicals for." These follow the pattern set by the recently established and very useful free-floating subdivision "--Services for," which is utilized under "Blind." In the latter example, "Military lawyers" should be established as a subject, with a second subject assigned using the "--Lawyers" subdivision under an armed forces branch whenever the occasion warrants.

Still dealing with the same grouping of terms, "Art, Jewish" and "Architecture, Jewish" are headings established by LC. Except for the use of inversion, these two subjects make sense and are quite understandable. But some other situations in the discipline of art are problematic. Excluding for now any discussion of the difficulties created by inversion structure and the comprehension problems posed by "rival headings" (see B5 below), there are a number of art headings (and their analogs elsewhere) that have structural inconsistencies. The majority of art genres use the structure "[genre, cultural/geographical qualifier]," for instance, "Art, American," "Sculpture, Chinese," and "Painting, Dutch." The same genres also allow the structure "[genre--place]," for instance, "Art--United States," "Sculpture--China," and "Painting--Netherlands." A significant amount of other art genres use only the structure "[genre--place]," for instance, "Furniture--United States," "Glassware--Japan," and "Silverwork--Canada." Some art genres, in addition, allow the structure "[genre, non-cultural/non-geographical qualifier such as religion, period, or type]," for instance, "Art, Jewish," "Architecture, Jewish," "Antiques, Victorian," or "Furniture, Baroque."

To avoid being distracted too much by inversions at this point, we will arbitrarily eliminate all inversions. With the inversions gone, the three structural patterns mentioned above now become: "[cultural/geographical qualifier plus genre]," for example, "American art"; "[genre--place]," for example, "Furniture--United States"; and "[non-cultural/non-geographical qualifier plus genre]," for example, "Jewish architecture." The last-mentioned structure, which does not deal with geographical concepts, is easy to understand and does not get confused with the other types of headings. The first two, however, which deal with or imply geographical areas, have contradictory structures. The first structure, whether direct or inverted, presents the cultural group/geographical area in adjectival form, while the second structure presents the geographical area in the form of a noun. The first structure, furthermore, includes the cultural/geographical concept in the primary structural element while the second includes it in the first subordinate structural element or subdivision.

In addition, the fact that some genres can be represented by two different structures, for example, the above-mentioned example "Sculpture, Chinese" versus "Sculpture--China," demonstrates the degree of structural confusion. (It should be noted that LC intended that these two structures serve two different semantic purposes, but it will be shown later that doubt can be cast on the effectiveness of this dual semantic purposes policy.) Even making the headings more structurally rational and sound by elimination of inversions does not at all help these patterns. For many headings, the change from an inverted form to a direct form performs structural wonders. But such is not the case here. The structure is so markedly inconsistent that it is difficult to defend. Finally, note that all the structural examples utilized in the explication of this principle and the previous one were ultimately derived from the subject "Lawyers." This illustrates that one does not have to peruse the entire list of LC subject headings to discover a sampling of headings with faulty structure. Examples are commonplace.

3. The relationship between structural elements in LC subject headings must be logical

One of the factors which contributes most to the genius of LC subject headings is the "logical string" concept developed by LC. "Logical strings" is this author's terminology for the structure employed whenever one or more subordinate structural elements/subdivisions are added to a primary structural element, with all structural elements connected by double dashes (--). Some examples of logical strings:

Shakespeare, William, 1564-1616--Style
Chinese--New York (N.Y.)
Canada--Politics and government--1980-
Agriculture--Economic aspects--Indonesia--Java
Aged--Services for--Japan--Tokyo--Evaluation
Education--France--Paris--History--Bibliography--Catalogs
Furniture--England--Collectors and collecting--Illinois--Chicago--History

These and countless other logical strings are excellent devices for subject access to any concept which cannot be totally represented by a primary structural element. Or, in other words, they take care of the more complex topics. Part of the beauty of logical strings is their extreme flexibility. This very valuable flexibility, however, does not mean that the structural elements can be assembled in any random fashion. Their order, as well as the vocabulary of the subdivisions, has been well controlled by LC in recent years by their establishment of comprehensive and detailed subdivision lists along with good guidelines as to their usage.[5] Since there are a variety of possible structures which a logical string can take, it would be difficult if not impossible to provide general rules that cover all situations. Strict control of subdivision order and vocabulary, though, will preserve the integrity of logical strings.

There is one overall guideline, however, which should always be kept in mind in dealing with logical strings. As shown in the seven typical examples given above, logical strings tend to have a progression from broad concepts to more narrow concepts, though the pattern is somewhat irregularly applied. In some cases, for example, "History" will precede "19th century" and in other cases, "19th century" will precede "History." Theoretically, these irregularities are a structural problem, and really should be made universally consistent in pattern. On a practical basis, they can be tolerated as long as the patterns for each case are clearly presented in LC's subject heading listings (the "red books," their supplements, and their successors, plus the lists of subdivisions), and as long as the logical string serving the same type of heading is consistent in the order of the elements.

One practice which will help preserve the broader to narrower integrity of logical strings would be to retain the very successful "indirect" pattern for geographical subdivision used by LC for a number of years. (In 1987, LC proposed discarding the indirect pattern in favor of the "direct" pattern, but public opinion caused LC to stay, at least for a while, with indirect.[6]) The indirect pattern, as shown in the last four examples above, always places a larger geographical area before a smaller geographical area in the string. This is more logical than the direct pattern which eliminates one potential element in the string and combines, when applicable, the two geographical elements into one. With the direct pattern, there is a built-in structural inconsistency because localities such as "Toronto" can be in the same relative position as larger geographical areas such as "Ontario." In the last four examples above, the direct pattern would produce the following:

Agriculture--Economic aspects--Java (Indonesia)
Aged--Services for--Tokyo (Japan)--Evaluation
Education--Paris (France)--History--Bibliography--Catalogs
Furniture--England--Collectors and collecting--Chicago (Ill.)--History

The direct pattern definitely weakens the logical progression tendency of broad to narrow. And often the weakening occurs in the first subdivision, as in the "Education" example shown above, and thereby the weakening becomes more detrimental. Furthermore, the direct pattern potentially makes subject retrieval a little harder and/or time consuming. If a subject catalog (manual or online) is arranged in the direct pattern, the following type of arrangement ensues:

Botany--Baja California (Mexico)
Botany--Brazil
Botany--Cabo Rojo (Mexico)
Botany--California
Botany--Canada
Botany--Connemara (Ireland)
Botany--Jalisco (Mexico)
Botany--Latin America
Botany--Malaysia
Botany--Mexico

This very condensed sample, taken from a functioning catalog, illustrates that the four works on the botany of Mexico are separated from each other. Or, in other words, the advantages of collocation are lost. Whether the catalog is in card form or online, the separation or lack of collocation makes the retrieval of the four items more difficult, especially when the number of irrelevant entries intervening between each item are much more numerous than the limited illustration above. With the indirect pattern all the works on Mexico are adjacent. It could be argued that in one sense all occurrences of "Mexico" in a sophisticated online catalog are adjacent because the computer can retrieve the word no matter where it appears in headings. But although the computer may not need structured headings, human brains accustomed to LC and similar systems need the order and understandability provided by clear and consistent structure. Whether this will always be true is uncertain.

Furthermore, the indirect pattern does not negatively affect the retrieval of any locality, for example, Jalisco, Mexico, or Connemara, Ireland. No appreciable difference in time or knowledge is needed to access the item via the country followed by the locality than via the locality followed by the country. Additionally, anybody who wishes to access all the works on a topic which pertains to a larger geographical area such as a country, province, or state would have to search under all potential localities if the direct pattern is used. Altogether, the use of the direct pattern is less logical and less practical. It removes some of the logic from the logical strings and reduces the potential retrieval of the subject.

4. The structure of LC subject headings should support conversion into understandable and consistent diagrams

In the explication of the principle on consistency of structural elements in LC subject headings, some diagrams were employed to explain the structure. One valid test of the structural soundness of any system is whether the components of the system can stand up to the methodology of diagramming. The diagrams, in addition, must be clear and understandable and produce consistent results for similar purposes. A substantial amount of LC subject patterns, as suggested by the diagrams utilized previously, do not pass the test. If some of the type of art headings discussed above are fully diagrammed, their structural shortcomings become quite obvious. For example, the headings for art produced in Los Angeles and furniture work done in Los Angeles would be:

Art, American--California--Los Angeles
Furniture--California--Los Angeles

In this author's diagrams, the two headings would convert to:

[genre, cultural/geographical qualifier]--[non-local geographical area]--[local geographical area]
[genre]--[non-local geographical area]--[local geographical area]

It is quite apparent that these two similar-purpose headings do not have consistent diagrams. Even if the inversion in "Art, American" was eliminated, the structure would still prove to be inconsistent with the other pattern. "American art--California--Los Angeles" would diagram as:

[cultural/geographical qualifier plus genre]--[non-local geographical area]--[local geographical area]

To bring these disparate similar-purpose structures into line with each other, one of them has to be changed. The obvious candidate is the "Art, American" structure which on top of being an inversion has the more complex structure. If "Art, American" is altered to simply "Art," the subject heading becomes "Art--California--Los Angeles" and the diagram becomes "[genre]--[non-local geographical area]--[local geographical area]." (Note that "Art--California--Los Angeles" has long been established as a valid LC heading.) With that change of structure, the headings currently in the "Art, American" style would become completely compatible with the headings in the "Furniture--United States" style. In contrast to the above problems, many types of LC subject heading structures do support conversion into diagrams. Taking four examples of LC subject headings used in the explication of the principle about logical strings, two generic patterns are derived.

The two subjects

Chinese--New York (N.Y.)

and

Education--France--Paris--History--Bibliography--Catalogs

equate into the one generic diagram

[topic]--[non-local geographic area] (optional)--[local geographical area] (optional; if used, previous element must also be used)--[subdivisions in order prescribed] (optional)

Another two subjects

Agriculture--Economic aspects--Indonesia--Java

and

Aged--Services for--Japan--Tokyo--Evaluation

equate into the one generic diagram

[topic]--[subtopic]--[non-local geographical area] (optional)--[local geographical area] (optional; if used, previous element must also be used)--[subdivisions in order prescribed] (optional)

(In the first generic diagram remember that "New York (N.Y.)" like "Washington (D.C.)," "Berlin (Germany)" and "Jerusalem," is not treated as a local geographical area.[7]) Actually, all four of these subjects could be accommodated by a single "super generic" diagram:

[topic]--[subtopic] (optional)--[non-local geographical area] (optional)--[local geographical area] (optional; if used, previous element must also be used)--[subdivisions in order prescribed] (optional)

All of LC's subject headings should be put to this diagramming test and if similar-purpose headings do not have identical structural patterns, adjustments should be made to make the structures identical. The ultimate purpose of such diagramming, of course, is to improve subject heading structure and thereby, it is hoped, also improve subject access.

5. "Rival headings" must be eliminated from LC subject headings

The structure of the "Art, American" type headings has been previously demonstrated to be inconsistent with the structure of the similar-purpose "Furniture--United States" type headings. But what about the headings in the style "Art--United States" or "Art--California--Los Angeles"? As touched upon above, this type of heading is permitted under current LC policy in spite of the presence of the similar-appearing "Art, American" or "Art, American--California--Los Angeles" type headings. As alluded to before, LC designed these two seemingly redundant types of structure to have two different purposes. "Art, American" is intended to mean art produced in the United States or in American style, and similarly "Art, American--California--Los Angeles" is intended to mean art produced in Los Angeles or in the Los Angeles style. In comparison, "Art--United States" is intended to mean art of any type or style located in the United States, and similarly "Art--California--Los Angeles" is intended to mean art of any type or style located in Los Angeles. The subtle and not well understood differences of meaning between the two types of heading is not consistently comprehended by subject catalogers and probably is a source of confusion for most library users. It would not be surprising if most library users looked only under the "Art, American" type heading or only under the "Art--United States" type heading. Even if both types of heading are used as access points by most library users, it may well be that most library users do not understand and/or appreciate the relatively slight differences in purpose.

Therefore, these two types of headings strongly act as "rival headings." Or, in other words, they compete for the same concepts in the LC subject heading system. Such rivalry/competition should not be permitted. Since the "Art, American" style heading has already been shown to be inconsistent in structure with similar-purpose headings, as well as being an inversion, the "Art, American" type heading is the "rival heading" which should be eliminated. Note that "rivalry" situations for this type of heading are not limited to geographical areas. Whenever an ethnic group is located in or primarily confined to a specific geographical area, e.g., "Art, Maori" there is some potential for rivalry. In this case, using two headings, "Maoris" and "Art--New Zealand," would make subject access clearer. (Theoretically, the first subject should be "Maoris--Art" as is done for "Indians,"[8] but at present that structure is not allowed.)

The "Art--New Zealand" heading may be too broad for those who believe that headings have to be absolutely precise in their coverage. If that philosophy was injected into subject headings, a book on half the history of France would not be properly serviced by "France--History" or a book on mammals in several parts of Kentucky would not be properly serviced by "Mammals--Kentucky." If you analyze a large sample of LC headings assigned, you may well find that many if not most headings are at least somewhat broader than the item cataloged. But what is wrong with that? In some cases there is no convenient substitute, as in the "France--History" and "Mammals--Kentucky" examples. In other cases, such as the "Art--New Zealand" situation, eliminating the heading because it is to some degree too broad, yet in other ways suitable, is to eliminate an access point. One of the most consistent complaints about the application of LC subject headings has been not enough headings. Too many headings created by the liberal application of subjects, of course, can be a problem. But not enough headings, this author feels, is a much worse situation, and has been one of the failures of LC in the past.

Other types of headings also fall into the "rival headings" category. For instance, there is a group of LC headings with the pattern "[religion in adjectival form] art and symbolism." These include "Buddhist art and symbolism," "Islamic art and symbolism," and

"Jewish art and symbolism." At the same time, though, LC also has established the headings "Art, Buddhist," "Art, Islamic," and "Art, Jewish." To complicate the situation, the only heading established for Christian art as a general grouping is "Christian art and symbolism" and the only heading established for Hindu art as a general grouping is "Art, Hindu." So in this case the "rival headings" were mixed in with a clear case of inconsistency.

Two other examples of "rival headings" are the use of "Radio" versus "Radio broadcasting" and "Television" versus "Television broadcasting." In these two cases, however, both the involved terms are definitely needed. What has occurred with "Radio" and "Television," in contrast to other situations, is a partial rivalry. Since "Radio" and "Television" can both be subdivided geographically, as can both "Radio broadcasting" and "Television broadcasting," the two sets of headings can compete with each other especially if the cataloger does not carefully examine all headings in the two areas. This potential for rivalry is increased by LC's interweaving of broadcast terms with equipment terms. Under "Radio," the broadcast terms "--Censorship," "--Competitions," "--Jamming" (as a cross reference), and "--Law and legislation" are printed. Under "Television," the broadcast terms "--Law and legislation," "--Lighting," "Production and direction," "--Psychological aspects," and "--Stage-setting and scenery" are printed. Partial "rival headings" like the ones in "Radio" and "Television" are not as bad theoretically as the pure rival headings, but they can be equally as deceptive and equally as damaging to good subject access.

6. *Inversions should be strongly avoided in LC subject headings*

Headings of the type "Art, American" have previously been discussed and theoretically discarded for structural inconsistency and for inability to support consistent diagramming. In this section, the "Art, American" style headings are given the third strike and are out.

The fundamental reason, apparently, why LC established inversions was to promote collocation. That is, they felt that inverting terms would help bring related terms together in the catalog by putting the noun first, for example, chemistry and short stories, followed by the adjective or other words. There are two difficulties with this mode of thinking. First, in the case of terms like "Chemistry, Organic" or "Short stories, German," it could well be debated whether "organic" or "chemistry" should be the collocation point or whether "German" or "short stories" should be the collocation point. Second, inversions have not been universally created, partly because of shifting policies over the years. Therefore, the confusing dichotomy of "German fiction" versus "Short stories, German" and myriad other examples has come into being. (If all reasonably invertible terms had been inverted, the use of inversions would have a degree of justification.) In addition, many inversions were created (not necessarily consciously) as a substitute for developing subdivisions, for instance, "Employees, Training of" and "Pregnancy, Complications of." These points will be discussed further below.

The negative factors which cause the total theoretical rejection of "Art, American" as an individual case and all inversions as a group are two in number. First, as already hinted at, inversions are structurally unsound. In addition to the reasons previously given, inversions are inherently awkward. In situations such as "Wood carving, Mbembe (Cross River African people)" which combines inversion with "rivalry" potential and over-complexity, or the double inversion "Aged, Writings of the, French-Canadian," they become extremely clumsy.

Second, inversions are linguistically unnatural. Normally, we do not talk or write using inversions. The only significant exception is the frequent inversion of personal names on listings, applications, etc. This exception is reflected in LC's inversion of most personal names as access points. Overall, there appears to be no valid reason for the general retention of inversions. Some individual cases may prove to be supportive of the inversion structure, but as a whole, inversions should be eliminated.

There are two general ways inversions can be converted. The first is to simply alter the inverted form to a direct or uninverted form. This method applies to headings such as "Chemistry, Organic," "Psychology, Pathological," "Michigan, Lake," "Art, Modern," and "Art, Jewish," which would become "Organic chemistry," "Pathological psychology," "Lake Michigan," "Modern art," and "Jewish art." The second is to simplify the structure of the primary structural element by eliminating at least one word, and to include the eliminated concept in the subdivisions. LC has used this technique to change some headings in recent years, for example, "Teachers, Self-rating of" to "Teachers--Self-rating of," so the methodology has been proven to be valid and useful.

Which of the two conversion options should be exercised in any situation depends on the total context of the heading to be converted. The previously much-discussed "Art, American" heading, if changed to "Art--United States" type headings, would be using the second option. That option would be selected because of the many genres such as "Furniture," "Handicraft," and "Jewelry" which have the identical structure as "Art--United States," and also because using the first option to produce "American art" does not remove the rivalry with "Art--United States." In contrast, though, "Short stories, American" and other identically-structured headings in the field of literature should be changed by means of the first option. Since the largest proportion of literary genres have the structure "[cultural/geographical qualifier plus genre]," for example, "Indonesian literature," "French poetry," and "Mexican drama," forms like "Short stories, American," "Proverbs, Danish," and "Satire, Brazilian" should be altered to the same structure. By doing that, the three examples would become "American short stories," "Danish proverbs," and "Brazilian satire." If there are any reservations about eliminating inversions because of the fear that access would be reduced because significant terms such as "Short stories" or "Proverbs" will no longer be at the beginning, scrupulous employment of see-references will assure integrity of access. After all, whether the subject is in direct order or inverted, see-references would normally be made anyway. It should be noted, in conclusion, that LC in recent years has been tending to avoid establishment of inverted headings and in addition has changed some inversions to a direct form, for example, "Tales, French" to "Tales--France." The computer, of course, is in large part responsible for this trend.

7. "Reverse patterns" should not be permitted in LC subject headings

"Reverse patterns" are those LC subject headings which have an opposing structure to similar-purpose headings. One reverse pattern is "Embryology--Birds [Crustacea, Insects, etc.]" which has the structural diagram "[Function or characteristic--Organism]." Using the case of "Birds," other headings of similar purpose are "Birds--Cytology," "Birds--Physiology," "Birds--Reproduction," etc. These all have the diagram "[Organism--Function or characteristic]." Another reverse pattern is "Satellites--Jupiter [Mars, Saturn, etc.]," which has the structural diagram "[Characteristic--Astronomical body]." Using the case of "Mars," other headings of similar purpose are "Mars (Planet)--Atmosphere," "Mars (Planet)--Geology," "Mars (Planet)--Orbit," etc. These all have the diagram "[Astronomical body--Characteristic]."

Such cases not only contradict the pattern of the majority of their relatives, but "reverse patterns" in addition place the least important aspect, the function or characteristic, in the dominant initial structural element position, and the most important aspect, the organism or astronomical body, in the subordinate subdivision position. In every case of LC subject heading usage, the most important element should be first. (It could be debated in these cases as to which is the most important element, the thing or the characteristic. But because the characteristic is always completely dependent on the existence of the thing, and the reverse is not always true, the thing has to be regarded as dominant. Anyway, both the thing and the characteristic can be accessed by the computer if properly structured.) Since there appears to be no valid reason to sustain "reverse patterns," and since LC is apparently no longer establishing them, these awkward and structurally-inconsistent patterns should be abandoned. For the examples discussed above, "Embryology" and "Satellites," the reverse patterns can be eliminated simply by making "Embryology" and "Satellites" free-floating subdivisions, for instance, "Frogs--Embryology" and "Saturn (Planet)--Satellites."

There is a precedent for this type of conversion. In 1985, LC completely changed another "reverse pattern" when they abandoned the "city flip" provision.[9] Before the "city flip," conflicting patterns such as "Airports--Illinois" versus "Chicago Metropolitan Area (Ill.)--Airports" were allowed. After the "city flip," the above examples both attained identical structure, that is, "Airports--Illinois" and "Airports--Illinois--Chicago Metropolitan Area." If structural reversals of major proportions like the "city flip" can be made, then other "reverse patterns" existing in the LC subject heading system can be similarly corrected.

8. In LC subject headings, topics should have precedence over places as initial structural elements except for some broad inherently historical, socio-economic, and cultural concepts

As suggested by the reference to the broad to narrow tendencies of logical strings and in the discussion of "reverse patterns," the most important or basic aspect of a subject should be the primary or initial structural element. The most problematical aspect of this concept are the headings which have geographical areas as the initial structural element. In many cases, such as "Airports" and other topics involved in the "city flip" situation mentioned above, geographical areas have been improperly established as initial structural elements. Such situations are contrary to the premise of important elements first and are in addition a type of "reverse pattern."

Up to 1987, one example of improper placement of geographical areas as the initial element was [Place--Public buildings]. In 1987, LC wisely converted that pattern to "[public buildings--place],"[10] thus strengthening their general pattern of making topics the initial structural element rather than places. This pattern should be rigorously maintained, with the exception of those broad inherently historical, socio-economic, or cultural concepts for which LC has established period subdivisions under places or which serve as links with other places. The excepted concepts include "Civilization," "Commerce," "Description and travel," "Economic conditions," "Foreign relations," "History," "Military relations," "Politics and government," "Relations," "Religion," "Social conditions," and "Social life and customs."

There are three general reasons for having the geographical area as the initial structural element in these cases. The first is the matter of practicality, since countless headings have been applied using this pattern. The second is the advantage of having period subdivisions appropriate to the specific place established under various subdivisions. The third is the lack of any real theoretical support for having the concept instead of the place as the initial element. Certainly, some concepts such as "History" which is a valid subdivision under topics, and "Economic conditions," "Politics and government," and "Social conditions" which have the analogs "Economic aspects," "Political aspects," and "Social aspects" as valid subdivisions under topics, have some theoretical support as subdivisions rather than initial elements because of the consistency factor. (The same also applies to a similar set of analogs "Economic conditions," "Political activity," and "Social conditions" which are valid subdivisions under specified groups of persons.) And somehow these four broad concepts as well as "Civilization," "Description and travel," and "Social life and customs," because they are so basic to the place involved, seem to be very ill-at-ease as initial structural elements when associated with a geographical area.

Those topics, in addition, which function as links with other places, for example, "Commerce" and "Foreign relations," are superior as subdivisions rather than initial elements for sound practical reasons if not for theoretical reasons. "France--Commerce--Italy" and "United States--Foreign relations--India" are far more valuable headings than anything which could be devised by making "Commerce" and "Foreign relations" initial structural elements subdivided by place. (Theoretically, if geographical subdivision is made completely flexible as will be suggested in E6 below, "Commerce--[place]" used for each area, and "Foreign relations--[place]" used for each area could adequately cover the concepts. But the linking feature and the "logical pairs" device which results [see E5 below] are so very effective and understandable that such a structure is definitely preferred when possible.) On the other hand, it could be argued that "Race relations" or "Population," which are used as subdivisions under places, may be better as initial structural elements because they are not among the absolutely basic concepts inherent in a place, have not had period subdivisions established, and do not have the practical function of serving as links between geographical areas.

Overall, although there is no clear theoretical mandate for doing so, the most basic historical, socio-economic and cultural concepts associated with geographical areas should be subordinate to the geographical areas. The justification for this view may only be intuition, but the opposing view is not really supported by any firm theoretical foundations either. Whenever the situation of a geographical area as the initial structural element can be substantially doubted, the topic should be converted to the initial structural element. Only a small core of fundamental topics, which do not "feel right" or function well as initial elements, plus those topics which serve well as links, should be treated as subordinate to geographical areas and therefore be subdivisions under places.

One might note that this principle could be interpreted as being somewhat contradictory to the very important tenet of consistency. Because the principle allows for geographical areas to be either initial elements or subdivisions depending on the nature of the topic, a definite degree of inconsistency is present. But what are the alternatives? Making the place consistently the initial element violates the principle of most important element first in so many cases. Making the topic consistently the initial element would be inconsistent with those non-geographic area situations where the same topic is used as a subdivision. For example, "History--Africa" would be inconsistent with "Education--History." In any case, the proposal in this principle is no worse than the current reality of LC which is inconsistent. The principle recognizes that without drastic restructuring, a compromise solution, albeit involving inconsistency, is the only realistic alternative. Pure solutions don't always work in real life.

9. New structural concepts/relationships for the LC subject heading system should be explored

Up to this point, all discussions of structure have dealt with examples of structure already established by LC. But LC subject headings should not be necessarily restricted to those structural concepts already developed. Other structural options should be seriously considered. For example, a recently-proposed idea suggests using a slash between two subjects which have a relation to each other in the item being cataloged.[11] If, for instance, the item is on the interrelationship of marriage and alcoholism, the relational device proposed would produce the one subject "Marriage/Alcoholism" instead of the two subjects "Marriage" and "Alcoholism." In all such cases, a mirror heading, for instance, "Alcoholism/Marriage" would also be applied.

If this type of structure is unconditionally permitted, an enormous amount of useful and flexible headings would be potentially available. Not only would there be the capability to link any two separate primary structural elements, but certain types of existing headings which somewhat awkwardly combine two concepts could be eliminated. Dual concept headings such as "Science and Civilization," "Parent and Child," "Cats in Art," "Motor ability in children," and "Communication in science" could be very effectively converted to "Science/Civilization," "Parents/Children," "Cats/Art," "Motor ability/Children," and "Communication/Science." The clumsiness of the dual concept would be gone in all these "[topic]/[topic]" situations, and in addition each of the partners in the slash relationship would be expressed in the same terminology which is used when they are not in the slash relationship. (If the slash is not satisfactory, perhaps a colon could be substituted as the relational punctuation.)

Note that the similarly awkward structure "[topic] as [topic]," for instance, "Children as musicians," was not employed as an example above. The reason for the exclusion was that "[topic] as [topic]" headings are not relational like the other types. In essence, "[topic] as [topic]" could just as meaningfully be expressed as "[topic] = [topic]," for the concepts in some way overlap or have a sort of indirect equality. For example, "Children as musicians" really means that the children and the musicians are the same entities. Similarly, the dual concept heading "Women lawyers," which is just a semantically streamlined version of the former heading "Women as lawyers," really means that the women and the lawyers are the same entities. So both "Children as musicians" and "Women lawyers" could be changed to the structure "[topic] = [topic]" or "Children = Musicians" and "Women = Lawyers."

Furthermore, both the "[topic]/[topic]" and the "[topic] = [topic]" structures can very readily have any type of subdivision, including geographical areas, attached to them. They would in all ways function in the same manner as current headings. For example, "Marriage/Alcoholism--United States," "Cats/Art--Catalogs," and "Women=Lawyers--United States--Biography" would be quite useful headings.

The punctuation, of course, is only for the human eye, to give structure and meaning to the headings. The computer usually ignores punctuation and so it would be necessary to insert some kind of tag, similar to the x, y, and z presently used in the MARC system, to service the punctuation. With such tags inserted in the proper places, the three headings mentioned in the previous paragraph could be retrieved online as follows:

Marriage/Alcoholism--United States
Marriage
Alcoholism
Marriage/Alcoholism
Alcoholism/Marriage
Marriage--United States
Alcoholism--United States
Marriage/Alcoholism--United States
Alcoholism/Marriage--United States
Cats/Art--Catalogs
Cats
Art
Cats/Art
Art/Cats
Cats--Catalogs
Art--Catalogs
Cats/Art--Catalogs
Art/Cats--Catalogs
Women=Lawyers--United States--Biography
Women
Lawyers
Women=Lawyers
Lawyers=Women

Women--United States
Women--Biography
Lawyers--United States
Lawyers--Biography
Women = Lawyers--United States
Lawyers = Women--United States
Women = Lawyers--Biography
Lawyers = Women--Biography
Women = Lawyers--United States--Biography
Lawyers = Women--United States--Biography

What great flexibility could be attained with these structural innovations, especially when more complex topics such as "Marriage (Hindu law)," "Longhair Cats," "Art, Medieval," "Single women," or "Lawyers, Foreign" could be substituted for the simpler topics "Marriage," "Cats," "Art," "Women," or "Lawyers" used in the above examples. Add to this the possibility of using two slashes, or an equal sign plus a slash, for example, "Marriage/Alcoholism/Crime" instead of "Marriage" plus "Alcoholism and Crime," and "Women = Lawyers/Literature" instead of "Women in literature" plus "Women lawyers" plus "Lawyers in literature," and the flexibility seems endless. Some headings such as the "Marriage/Alcoholism/Crime" example may be vague and potentially ambiguous, but the LC system presently contains much vagueness and ambiguity and such characteristics will probably always be present in the system or any other subject retrieval system of wide scope and great complexity. Perfect comprehensibility and perfect fit of subject terms with the item being cataloged is an ideal seldom achieved. The advantage of this proposal is that it allows for consistent and succinct presentation of all subject concepts involved, plus enables enormous computer flexibility. And at the same time many and perhaps all awkward dual concepts would be purged from LC's subject heading system. These new structural concepts/relationships and similar structural modifications which may be proposed should be reviewed, tested, and adopted if they improve the theoretical bases and/or practical retrieval of LC subject headings.

C. Terminology

1. Natural language must be used as much as possible in LC subject headings

Natural language, that is, the everyday, commonly-used language of reasonably educated persons, should be fully utilized in the LC subject heading system. Choice of terminology, grammar, and spelling are all involved under the umbrella of natural language. And when LC subject headings are utilized in cultures and languages other than North American and English, cultural and linguistic factors must be given the highest consideration in the formulation of subject heading terminology. In all cultures and languages, overly academic, overly formal, overly obsolete, or artificial terminology should be avoided if feasible. (Terminology must, if possible, be satisfactory for the needs of both the specialist and the generalist.) On the other hand, since natural language frequently uses the same word for different purposes, there are of course situations where parenthetical qualifiers or other devices which do not occur naturally must be employed to distinguish identical terms from each other. For instance, "Interest," "Interest (Law)," "Interest (Philosophy)," "Interest (Psychology)," and "Reward (Ethics)," "Reward (Law)," "Reward (Psychology)," "Reward (Theology)," are two sets of such headings involving common and familiar terms.

With the exception of these qualifiers and other needed devices, LC as a whole uses natural language and has been increasing this tendency in recent years. There are some terms, for instance, "Communication and traffic," "Sweating system," and "Clothing and dress" which perhaps never fell into the category of natural language. There are also some terms, such as "Moving-pictures," which were probably valid natural language phraseology at one time but which have long been obsolete and in this era run counter to the natural language theorem. When "Moving-pictures" was recently converted to "Motion pictures,"[12] it not only indicated LC's willingness to update a heading which no longer uses natural language, but it showed common sense as well. They could have chosen "Film" as the heading, but since "Film" would have to receive a parenthetical qualifier due to the several varying uses of the term, the choice of "Motion pictures" was more valid because of the natural language principle. Overall, natural language must be the key factor in determining choice of terms in LC subject headings.

2. Consistent and clearly understood terminology must be used in LC subject headings

Although natural language must be used as much as possible in LC subject headings, it is equally as important that similar purpose headings are consistent in their terminology and that the terminology be clearly understood. One major subject area with both inconsistent and unclear terminology (as well as inconsistent structure) is LC's overall approach to the name form for literatures. Some examples:

1. "German literature--Switzerland" and "Swiss literature (German)" both mean German Swiss literature, while German literature in Austria is represented by "German literature--Austrian authors."
2. "Malay literature" is used for the dominant literature of the country of Malaysia, but "Malaysian literature" should be used instead since "Malay literature" has a much broader presence than in just the one nation.
3. Until recently, "American literature" and "Indonesian literature" were ambiguous, meaning both the dominant literatures of their respective nations and the collective literatures of their nations. As is indicated below, LC has created their solution to this dilemma, but their alternative is probably not well understood by users.
4. "Scottish literature" has a similar problem, meaning both literature in the Scottish dialect and the collective literatures of Scotland.
5. In contrast to the above two examples, "Philippine literature" means only the collective literatures of that country.
6. "African literature (English)" and "African literature (French)" are used by LC, but Arabic literature in Africa as a whole gets the subject "Arabic literature--Africa."

These inconsistencies and unclear situations can be rectified by: establishing the name of each literature which is dominant in a country, or which is in the national language, under forms which reflect the name of the country; establishing the names of national literatures which use multinational/transnational languages under forms which reflect the name of the nation; establishing literatures clearly specified with the names of multi-nation regions under forms which reflect the name of the region; adding parenthetical qualifiers for a particular literature whenever there is a potential conflict; and establishing a "multilingual" category for each nation or region which at all needs it, and in the style "[adjectival form of nation or region] literature (Multilingual)." With these principles, the above problems would have the following arrays of name forms:

Swiss literature (French)
Swiss literature (German)
Swiss literature (Italian)
Swiss literature (Multilingual)
Austrian literature [meaning the dominant literature in German]
Austrian literature (Multilingual)
Malaysian literature [meaning the dominant literature in Malay]
Malaysian literature (Chinese)
Malaysian literature (English)
Malaysian literature (Multilingual)
Malaysian literature (Tamil)
American literature [meaning the dominant literature in English]
American literature (French)
American literature (German)
American literature (Multilingual)
American literature (Spanish)
Indonesian literature [meaning the dominant literature in Indonesian]
Indonesian literature (Dutch)
Indonesian literature (Multilingual)
Scottish literature (English)

Scottish literature (Gaelic)
Scottish literature (Multilingual)
Scottish literature (Scottish dialect)
Philippine literature (English)
Philippine literature (Multilingual)
Philippine literature (Spanish)
African literature (Arabic)
African literature (English)
African literature (French)
African literature (Multilingual)
African literature (Portuguese)

Literatures of a subnational character, nondominant national literatures, or multinational/transnational literatures not affiliated with a particular nation are entered under their normal name forms, for example, "Arabic literature," "Basque literature," "Gaelic literature," "Hindi literature," "Javanese literature," "Latin literature," "Persian literature," and "Slavic literature."

It should be noted that LC has recently developed a method to take care of the "Multilingual" situation in some countries. LC has begun to add the subdivision "--Literatures" to the name of several nations, for example, "China--Literatures," "Indonesia--Literatures," and "United States--Literatures." Although this change was an improvement over the previous technique, it is not nearly as valid as the "Multilingual" solution proposed above. First, the "Multilingual" method can be applied freely to all literatures and all genres, as can all aspects of the above proposal. Second, use of the form "______ literature (Multilingual)" allows for the addition of standard period subdivisions as will be suggested below in D3, and the addition of the subdivision "--History and criticism." Third, LC's method makes it necessary to print the subdivision "--Literatures" in all applicable cases. Fourth, the structure "[place]--Literatures" violates the "topic as initial structural element" principle elaborated above in B8.

Another example of unclear terminology is "Local finance" versus "Finance, Public." The former term means public finance at the local level, but cannot be subdivided by specific localities. Instead, "Finance, Public" must be used whenever specific localities are involved. Therefore, public finance in Chicago would have the heading "Finance, Public--Illinois--Chicago," while public finance in Chicago plus several other Illinois localities would have the heading "Local finance--Illinois." Since both terms are quite valid, they both must be part of LC's main subject heading listing. However, if "Local finance" is treated only as a general concept, and not as relating to specific geographical areas, the situation of unclear terminology would be resolved.

3. Terminology in LC subject headings must be sensitive to social issues and other potentially delicate matters, but at the same time "trendy" terminology must be avoided

When the terminology for any LC subject heading dealing with social issues and any other possibly sensitive areas is being chosen, two dictums should be followed. First, neutral or descriptive terms must be preferred over terms which may have a negative tint to them. LC in recent years has been following this policy fairly well, although it apparently is not an explicitly-stated policy. For example, in relation to various ethnic groups, they have been changing the word "tribe," which definitely implies primitivism, to the completely neutral word "people."

Second, neutral or descriptive terms must be preferred over socially "trendy" terms. LC again has generally and implicitly obeyed this dictum, but has been sometimes inconsistent. Two recent decisions by LC illustrate their failure to follow a clear pattern. On one occasion, LC decided to stay with the established neutral term "Aged" instead of changing to the trendy term "Senior citizens." On another occasion LC decided to retain the long-standing descriptive term "Homosexuals" rather than change to the much less established term "Gays," but subsequently changed its mind and decided in favor of "Gays."[13] This flip-flop goes against the grain of history, and perhaps future events will dictate yet another change and thus again disrupt consistency and continuity.

On the other hand, LC in recent years has tended to treat social movements and cultural phenomena responsibly by establishing such headings as "Senior power," "Pro-choice movement," "Pro-life movement," "Gay liberation movement," and "Gay bars." For all of these five headings established by LC, there were no really equivalent terms already in effect. In addition, the situations described are not necessarily of a continuing long-range nature such as "Aged" and "Homosexuality." So in the matter of potentially delicate issues, a combination of sensitivity and a sense of history should be utilized to select terminology which is neither demeaning, insulting, nor faddish.

4. Disciplines and topics must be clearly differentiated in LC subject headings

One of the major areas of confusion in both the LC subject heading system and its application is the differentiation between disciplines and topics, particularly in the social sciences. In some cases, LC has provided clear scope notes separating disciplines from topics, for example:

Archaeology versus Antiquities
Economics versus Economic Conditions
Political Science versus Politics and Government
Public Administration versus Politics and Government
Sociology versus Social Conditions

They even have provided such scope notes for very specific situations, for instance, "United States--Economic conditions" and "United States--Politics and government."

Yet there is a problem with these because they require scope notes. Later on (in section E3), the disadvantages of scope notes and why they should be eliminated will be discussed in detail. If we presume for the present situation the elimination of long scope notes and the substitution of shorter "instructions," the five situations above, and others, can be serviced by putting under the discipline the instruction "[Theoretical discipline; use ______ under places for descriptions/history of situations/processes/institutions]." Utilizing the third item listed above as an example, the result would be:

Political science
[Theoretical discipline; use Politics and government under places for descriptions/history of situations/processes/institutions]

Not only would this method do the task in less space, but it actually provides more information, for instance, that the subdivision "Politics and government" can mean the history of the topic and therefore the subdivision "History" is not to be added after "Politics and government." Since "History" is never used under any of the above subdivision examples, this additional data is quite helpful. Another device that will aid in the differentiation between topic and discipline can be used in those cases where LC has not separated the two and uses the same term for both. Three such terms are "Anthropology," "Ethnology," and "Social psychology." When followed by a geographical subdivision, these terms can mean both the discipline in the place and the situation/processes/institutions in the place. Since the terms for the two different purposes are identical, it is necessary to distinguish one purpose from the other by listing the term twice and adding the parenthetical qualifier "(Discipline)" to the second one. Two examples of this device are:

Anthropology
Anthropology (Discipline)
Social psychology
Social psychology (Discipline)

In these cases, because the terms are adjacent and the discipline is clearly separated from the topic, no scope notes or instructions are needed.

Perhaps the most problematic instance of the mixing of discipline and topic is "Crime and criminals," which covers criminal activity, persons committing crimes, and the discipline of criminology. This situation can be resolved by the conversion of "Crime and criminals" into three headings, "Crime," "Criminals," and "Criminology." These three terms are sufficiently distinctive that instructions should not be needed, but if it is felt that the topic "Crime" should be more clearly differentiated from the discipline "Criminology," an instruction similar to the one used in the "Political science" illustration above will suffice:

Criminology
 [Theoretical discipline; for criminal activity use Crime]

The above example is probably unnecessary, and in fact does look like "overkill" or even a bit silly, but it does illustrate that short instructions can be used in just about any situation. As a whole, though, the more the LC subject heading system can be developed to avoid the need for special instructions, the better it will be. Note that the instruction in this case does not preclude the addition of the subdivision "History" nor of further period subdivisions such as "19th century." (More on the use of this type of period subdivision later in section D3.)

The discipline versus topic problem, of course, is not just confined to the social sciences. Another example of this conflict can be found with the term "Philology." In different places in LC's main subject heading listing (the "red books," their supplements and their successors), "Philology" is defined as a discipline and as the combined treatment of language and literature. (The *Subject Cataloging Manual* does not deal with the issue.) Accordingly, "French philology" could mean the discipline of studying both French language and French literature and/or the results of research on both French language and French literature. To avoid this lack of clarity and double meaning, "Philology" and its derivatives such as "French philology," "Classical philology," and "Chinese philology" should only apply to the discipline. For results of research on both language and literature, the term "______ philology" should not be used, but instead both "______ language" and "______ literature" should be used. The confusion in "Philology" could be avoided by adding an instruction under the discipline, similar to the above examples:

French philology
: [Theoretical discipline; for the results of research on French language and literature combined, use both French language and French literature]

Overall, the problems of discipline versus topic could be resolved by either adding a parenthetical qualifier to the term for the discipline when both discipline and topic employ the same term, or by putting a bracketed short instruction under the term for the discipline when the discipline and topic employ different terminology.

Such techniques will significantly increase the clarity of LC's subject heading listings (the main listing plus subdivision lists), and will in addition facilitate the consistent application of subject headings.

5. Name forms of persons, places, and organizations must remain the same whether main entry, added entry, or subject, except that governmental organizations of different chronological periods may have varying name forms

One of the oddest inconsistencies of terminology in the LC subject heading system is the occasional deviation of some geographical names from the general pattern. First, it must be clearly understood that there are two distinct functions of geographical names as subjects. One is their usage as topics or in 651, 650, 600, and 630 MARC tag subjects. The other is their usage as corporate bodies or in 610 tag subjects. As 651, 650, 600, or 630 topics, geographical names are always the same no matter what the chronological period. They always use the latest commonly-accepted form of name. If the name of the geographical area has remained stable over the years, like "Japan" or "France," the form used in 651, 650, 600, and 630 is the same as the form used in 610, 110, or 710. If the name has varied over the years, like "Sri Lanka" or "Soviet Union," the form used in 651, 650, 600, and 630 may or may not be the same as the form used in 610, 110, or 710. In this latter situation, the form in 651, 650, 600, and 630 will be the same as 610, 110, and 710 only if the latest commonly-accepted name form is valid for 610, 110, and 710 usage. That is, if the 610 subject deals with a noncurrent governmental entity, or the 110 or 710 entry reflects a noncurrent governmental entity, the name forms will be different from the 651, 650, 600, 630 topical subject name forms.

With this dual pattern in mind, it is hard to understand why LC exempts a few geographical areas from this pattern when treated as topical subjects. One example of this is "Papua New Guinea." Sometimes LC uses the current form "Papua New Guinea" and on other occasions the earlier forms "Papua" and/or "New Guinea (Territory)." The justification for this confusing dichotomy is that areas which have had significant territorial changes and varying forms of name should be assigned different name forms under certain conditions. When only "historical, political, or cultural" aspects of a geographical area are involved and an earlier historical period is being covered, one or more of the earlier forms of name are used. So if the events occurred prior to the Union of the Territory of Papua with the Territory of New Guinea in 1945, either "Papua" and/or "New Guinea (Territory)" is used. But when the "historical, political, or cultural" events occurred after 1945, or cover both the pre- and post-1945 periods, only "Papua New Guinea" is utilized. And when topics other than "historical, political, or cultural" aspects are involved, for instance, scientific, "Papua New Guinea" is always used.

"Malaysia" has a similarly questionable pattern. For "historical, political, and cultural" topics prior to the nation's independence in 1963 "Malaya" is used, and for all other aspects "Malaysia" is used. Yet LC directly contradicts itself here by printing in the main subject heading listing the heading "Malaya--History--Japanese occupation, 1942-1945," and by also printing in the 10th edition of the "red books" "World War, 1939-1945--Malaysia." (The latter heading was deleted in the 11th edition apparently for space reasons, but if it had been printed in the 11th edition one suspects that the form used in the 10th edition would have been repeated.) Both of these headings involve the same country and the same period, and both are "historical" in nature. In addition, LC sometimes uses the questionable pattern "[topic]--Malaysia--Malaya," for example, "Communism--Malaysia--Malaya," for works dealing entirely with mainland or peninsular Malaysia as opposed to the whole country, which consists of mainland Malaysia plus the two states of Sabah and Sarawak located on Borneo. Such misusage is comparable to not using "United States" when only the 48 contiguous states are involved.

Not only is the "historical, political, and cultural" rule potentially easy to misinterpret, sometimes misapplied, and theoretically unsound, LC has been inconsistent in their decisions as to which areas are affected by the rule. If all jurisdictions with "significant territorial changes" and historically varying names were treated in the same way, countries such as the United States, the Soviet Union, and India could also fall under the "historical, political, and cultural" rule. All three countries at one time or another had different names, with the Soviet Union changing names in this century. The United States and the Soviet Union have greatly expanded their territories in the past two centuries, and India has lost significant territory (Pakistan and Bangladesh) since World War II. Yet only one form of name is utilized for these nations in topical subject headings no matter what the historical period. It appears, therefore, that the segregation of areas like Papua New Guinea and Malaysia from the normal pattern for geographical areas is illogical and inconsistent. Although there may be some historical and cultural subtleties involved in the cases of Papua New Guinea and Malaysia, such is also true for many other geographical areas. In addition, it is doubtful that many catalogers or library users understand or appreciate the rationalization which dictates two or more name forms for the same geographical area. Accordingly, this LC practice should be abandoned.

6. Guidelines must be clearly established for formulating all types of subject heading terminology not specifically printed or clearly suggested in LC's subject heading documentation, AACR2, or LC's authority files

Not every potential subject heading can be printed in LC's subject heading publications, partly because of size considerations, and partly because it is quite impossible to know the name of every person, organization, place, chemical compound, biological organism, etc. Names of persons, organizations, and places, fortunately, are pretty well taken care of by LC's authority files and AACR2. And the *Subject Cataloging Manual* can be helpful in other cases. But in a few areas it is sometimes difficult to determine what terminology to use when the exact term does not appear in LC's subject heading documentation. Two guidelines which should be of help are given below.

A. *Unspecified literatures and literary genres*
When the terminology "______ language" or "______ dialect" appears in LC's main subject heading listing, but there is no corresponding term for literature, the term for literature ("______ literature") should be automatically

presumed. And when there is terminology (printed or presumed) for "______ literature" and/or one or more literary genres, for example, "______ poetry," the whole spectrum of literary genres plus the collective term for the literature, should be automatically presumed. So if only "______ drama" is established, "______ literature," "______ poetry," "______ fiction," "______ essays," etc., must also be considered as potentially valid.

B. *Unspecified chemical compounds and groupings*

When the terminology for a chemical compound or group of compounds, including minerals, does not appear in LC's main subject heading listing, the guidelines below can be used:

1) individual minerals and groups of minerals can be established under their most commonly known scientific name as determined by standard reference works;
2) individual inorganic compounds and groups of inorganic compounds can be established under their most commonly known scientific name as determined by standard reference works;
3) groups of organic compounds can be established under their most commonly known scientific name as determined by standard reference works;
4) individual organic compounds which have commonly known *and* simply expressed popular or scientific names can be established under these names, with the scientific name preferred;
5) individual organic compounds which do not have commonly known *and* simply expressed names can be covered by determining which element(s) other than carbon, hydrogen, and oxygen are in the compound, and by assigning one or more subjects from the series printed in LC's main subject heading listing with the form "Organo [element] compounds," for instance, "Organofluorine compounds" and "Organonitrogen compounds."

Part of the above guidelines are at least suggested by LC's main subject heading listing, but all of the above guidelines (or alternatives) should be clearly stated in LC subject heading policy.[14] The brief instruction given under "Chemistry, Organic" that "names of individual organic substances" are allowed as subjects is not very helpful in determining the exact form of name. Precise and specific guidelines for these two situations and any other similar terminology cases must be clearly established.

7. New concepts for expanding the effectiveness of LC's established terminology should be explored

LC uses a controlled vocabulary. Terms not part of the controlled vocabulary are linked to the controlled vocabulary by see references. But the present extent of see references is, as we all have experienced, far from adequate. A recent proposal,[15] if adopted in part or in whole, would greatly increase the effectiveness of the controlled vocabulary by creating an online "superthesaurus" of see references. The superthesaurus would be separate from the list of controlled vocabulary terms, and would contain an abundance of terms which could lead the user to the official LC term. Instead of having see reference access dependent on one or two or at best several terms, the implementation of the proposal would greatly enhance the user's potential for finding the exact term being searched for. This concept and any others which may make present terminology more useful should be given serious attention.

D. Specificity

1. Specificity and detail must be evenly and consistently developed throughout LC's subject heading listings

In recent years, LC has developed more specificity and detail (that is, narrowness) in their subject headings, largely through greater employment of subdivision. This is an excellent trend, and should be continued. But just as important as the development of specificity is the evenness and consistency of the details.

First, when similar purpose headings have uneven patterns of subdivision printed in LC's main subject heading listing, or have uneven structural relationships between the primary structural element and subdivisions, or unevenly allow the use of subdivision lists, corrective action should be considered. Second, when any heading clearly amenable to topical, geographical, and/or chronological subdivision is not so developed, or is only partially developed, the situation should be reviewed. Among the possible corrective actions are the following:

1. Missing topical subdivisions can be directly added to LC's main subject heading listing, or be inferred by allowing subdivision lists to be used;
2. If geographical subdivision is not present, and there is no clear and strong justification for not subdividing geographically, provision for such subdivision should be instituted. (One example of sufficient justification is when the heading is also used as a subdivision under places, for instance, "Cultural policy" or "Biography.") Geographical subdivision should be as universal as reason and logic dictate;
3. The use of chronological subdivision should be expanded beyond what LC now has developed. (The next two principles elaborate on increasing the development of historical period subdivisions.)

As a general rule, the decision between establishing more specificity and not doing so should normally fall on the side of more specificity. The world and its literature are not becoming less complex. Yet some libraries, for example, small public libraries, may prefer simpler, less complex headings with less detail. But LC still should provide for greater detail, for it is much easier for smaller libraries to delete parts of LC subject headings than for larger libraries to add to LC subject headings. Unless LC universally supplies two levels of subject headings similar to the multiple classification levels provided by Dewey classification, LC must continue to opt for fully-detailed headings and let those who choose less detail trim as desired. (Two levels of LC subject headings may be a good idea, but is perhaps a prohibitively expensive one. LC of course, would not do this for their collection, but they should consider doing this for the many other collections that use their subject headings. LC is showing increasing signs of taking the needs of others into account, and should continue this favorable trend.) Libraries who may decide to delete parts of LC subject headings for the sake of simplicity, however, may be cutting their own throats by adding to costs and by making more difficult any future shifts to greater complexity.

Similarly, libraries who opt for local or nonstandard alternatives for the sake of simplicity will loose the benefits of centralized and standardized cataloging as well as add to costs. On the other hand, it is understandable if libraries opt to use non-LC subject systems due to structural problems, unsatisfactory terminology, or poor presentation of data in the LC subject heading system. It is hoped, however, that LC's recent movement towards self-betterment, aided by external factors such as this publication, will produce a subject system which is of considerable value and utility to all types of libraries.

2. A full set of period subdivisions should be established for all significant geographical areas functioning as primary structural elements in LC subject headings

All significant geographical areas functioning as primary structural elements should have a full set of period subdivisions developed for them. That is, headings with the potential structure "[place]--[History, Economic conditions, Civilization, Relations, Politics and government, etc.]" should have available as complete a set of chronological subdivisions as can be justified. "Significant," of course, is a subjective term, but using the criteria of population and/or geographical size, historical or strategic importance, and the extent of literature, almost every nation, many multinational regions, and the more important and sizable subnational areas should fall under this umbrella. For every geographical primary structural element enhanced by period subdivisions, the five most basic concepts, "Description and travel," "Economic conditions," "History," "Politics and government," and "Social conditions" should always be covered, with other topics such as "Civilization," "Foreign relations," "Intellectual life," "Religion," and "Social life and customs" receiving chronological subdivision under the more significant geographical areas. And in every case all chronological periods from the earliest times to the present should be covered, with at least three period subdivisions established in most instances.

LC has developed a full set of needed period subdivisions under many areas, but for many other significant areas there are no period subdivisions or the subdivisions are incomplete or inconsistently applied. The apparent reasons for the lack, incompleteness, or inconsistency of period subdivision development are two in number. One is the supposed absence of a clear present need for period subdivision, or in other words, the amount of literature cataloged by LC does not justify subdivision by date. But for libraries with large or specialized collections, lack of period subdivisions can mean the necessity to search under many, even hundreds, of subjects to ferret out the ones with the appropriate chronological period. Also, some desired items may be missed because the period covered is not always evident from the title or other data. Even libraries with only one item in their catalog under, for example, "[place]--Economic conditions" will not be negatively affected if the heading were extended by "--1800-1918." (This presumes, of course, that the chronological coverage of the item was limited to this period.) To the contrary, the addition of the period subdivision provides the user with more complete and specific information which can be utilized or ignored depending on needs.

Providing period subdivisions before they are badly needed, that is, to have a policy of anticipation, is a wise course of action. There is a slight indication that LC is progressing toward a policy of anticipation in its overall subject heading development. It is hoped that this perceived trend will continue for period subdivision and other situations.

Reason number two derives from the opinion that things change so much and that establishing period subdivisions can be risky since they may have to be changed in the future. There is some validity in this viewpoint, for the economics and psychology of change must always be considered. But everything that is done is potentially subject to change, and subject headings are continually changing. In the long run, it is probably preferable to have reasonably good period subdivisions in place for everyday pragmatic use than to have possibly better period subdivisions which may be created in the uncertain future.

In summary, having more chronological specificity available to the library user, with the accompanying reduction of items to be searched, is a very beneficial policy which has very slight, if any, side effects.

3. Standard period subdivisions should be available for use, when appropriate, under all LC subject headings with a topic as the primary structural element

Similar to the development of period subdivisions under geographical primary structural elements whenever justified, a set of standard period subdivisions should be available for topical subject headings, that is, headings with topics as the primary structural element. LC has already partially filled this need by the establishment of the period subdivisions "16th century," "17th century," "18th century," "19th century," and "20th century" for use whenever headings with the structure "[topic]--History" are involved.[16] So if the item cataloged is about the history of French technology in the twentieth century, the resulting subject would be "Technology--France--History--20th century." These five period subdivisions can be universally used after the subdivision "--History" unless the primary structural element is a geographical area immediately followed by "--History," for example, "France--History," or unless LC has already established contradictory or conflicting period subdivisions under a topical subject, for example, "Education--China--History--1976-." The development of the five standard period subdivisions has considerably enhanced the specificity of LC subject headings. Further improvement could be achieved by adding another period subdivision, "To 1500," which would cover all of the period prior to the other five. If the topic warrants a more detailed breakdown in the medieval and/or ancient epochs, such specificity could be specially created under the topic.

The six standard period subdivisions could also be applied to another situation. LC has established some period subdivisions for use under "Authors, English." They are:

--Old English, ca. 450-1100
--Middle English, 1100-1500

--Early modern, 1500-1700
--18th century
--19th century
--20th century

In the *Subject Cataloging Manual*, LC implies that this type of pattern can be extended to other groups of literary authors.[17] But instead of dealing with this unclear directive, the six standard period subdivisions should be substituted for the six listed above for "Authors, English" and made universally applicable for all groups of literary authors. (Perhaps the subdivisions could also be applied to all groups of persons, for example, "Artists--France--19th century--Biography.") If the period prior to 1500 warrants a more detailed breakdown like in the case of "Authors, English," special provision can be made as suggested above for headings with the structure "[topic]--History."

One important subject area not covered by the set of standard period subdivisions is literature. Since literatures never use the subdivision "--History" but instead use the subdivision "--History and criticism," the set of standard period subdivisions does not apply. Many literatures have some period subdivisions established for the literatures as collective entities and/or for their individual genres such as fiction, drama, and poetry. But frequently the coverage is incomplete, with some kind of chronological gap present. "Hindi literature," for instance, has been assigned the following period subdivisions:

Hindi literature
--To 1500
--1500-1800
--20th century

Note that LC has not provided any subdivision for the 19th century, although LC has often established "--19th century" in other situations. In addition, LC has inconsistently applied period subdivisions to the individual genrès of a literature, frequently not providing period subdivisions for some genres and unevenly providing them in other cases. Again using Hindi literature, the following spotty period coverage has been established by LC:

Hindi drama
Hindi essays
Hindi fiction
Hindi letters
--1500-1800
Hindi poetry
--To 1500
--1500-1800
--20th century
Hindi prose literature

Furthermore, many literatures have absolutely no period subdivisions established under either the literature in general or the individual genres. To compensate for the missing/incomplete/inconsistent period subdivisions, the following set of standard period subdivisions should be applied to all living literatures, both individual and collective, whenever there is no conflict with existing headings:

--To 1800
--19th century
--20th century

The standard set can be used to fill in any gaps, such as the "--19th century" void for "Hindi literature." But when the literature in general and/or one or more of the individual genres has period subdivisions different from the standard set covering one or more of the time periods, like in the case of "Hindi literature" which has "--To 1500" and "1500-1800" assigned instead of "To 1800," the established subdivisions take precedence. Accordingly, a policy should be developed which automatically extends any period subdivisions established under the literature in general and/or any individual genre to all genres and to the literature in general. So for Hindi literature the set of three subdivisions established under Hindi literature in general and also under Hindi poetry should automatically be applied to all the genres. And with the "--19th century" gap being corrected by adopting the appropriate period from the standard set of three proposed above, Hindi literature in general and all its genres will be covered fully.

Perhaps a better overall approach to literature period subdivisions than is presently employed by LC should be considered. Instead of including period subdivisions under the literature in general and all its genres, only the literature in general should be so subdivided, and the following generic note should be supplied after every genre:

[For periods see ______ literature]

This method will make the handling of literary period subdivisions more rational and even-handed, and in addition will save space. So for our constant example, Hindi literature, the following would be established:

Hindi drama
  [For periods see Hindi literature]
Hindi literature
  --To 1500
  --1500-1800
  --19th century
  --20th century
Hindi prose literature
  [For periods see Hindi literature]
  [as well as others]

If a particular historical period is not valid for a particular genre, there would be no problem since the nonvalid period would never be applied and would not appear in print. For literatures which have no printed period subdivisions, it could be presumed that the standard set applies to the literature in general and to all genres in the same way that other sets of subdivisions apply to other situations. Therefore it would not be necessary to add any information. Slavic literature, for instance, would be treated like below:

Slavic drama
Slavic literature
Slavic poetry
[as well as others]

In effect, though, the following could be presumed:

Slavic drama
--To 1800
--19th century
--20th century
Slavic literature
--To 1800
--19th century
--20th century
Slavic poetry
--To 1800
--19th century
--20th century
[as well as others]

This scenario can occur in spite of LC's current establishment of two period subdivisions, "--To 1800" and "--20th century," under "Slavic literature," and one period subdivision "--To 1800" under "Slavic poetry." Since a full set of period subdivisions has not been established, it can be presumed that the standard set of three would apply and therefore it would not be necessary to print the period subdivisions. Accordingly, under the proposed new approach, incomplete sets of literary period subdivisions covered by the standard set of three would never be printed. In fact, incomplete sets of literary period subdivisions would not exist in LC's main subject heading listing. There would be either a full set of periods as in the case of "Hindi literature," or a reference to a full set as in the case of "Hindi drama," or no period subdivisions with the presumption of the application of the standard set as in the cases of "Slavic literature" and "Slavic poetry."

For those situations where the full set of three standard period subdivisions are not suitable for the history of a specific living literature, "To 1800" or both "To 1800" and "--19th century" could be deleted. For example:

Flemish literature
--19th century
--20th century

Nigerian literature (English)
--20th century

The subdivision "--20th century" by itself may seem to be redundant for those literatures existing only in the twentieth century, but in a relatively small amount of years "--21st century" will be valid for all living literatures. When that happens, the standard set of three period subdivisions will increase to four.

In summary, the two broad concepts elaborated above, that is, the period subdivision policy developed by LC (as modified and extended by this author) and the suggestions concerning period subdivisions for literature proposed by this author, probably accommodate all important topical subject heading situations not already specifically covered in LC's subject heading lists. At the least, no major exceptions have been noted by this author. But if the two concepts do not take care of all circumstances, other methods must be devised for any uncovered situations so that the widest possible provision for period subdivision usage is developed throughout the LC subject heading system.

E. Presentation of Data

1. Presentation of data in the LC subject heading system must be clear, consistent, complete, and concise; it also should be given at the point of primary contact

It is not enough to have sound structure, effective terminology, and adequate specificity in LC subject headings. The presentation of data in the LC subject heading system, that is, how subject headings and their usage are communicated to the cataloger and library patron, is also very important. Sound structure, effective terminology, and adequate specificity can, however, provide an environment which facilitates the goal of clear, consistent, complete, and concise presentation of data. When a system is logically constructed, semantically excellent, and fully developed, it is much easier to explain and understand. But even if these positive characteristics are present, it does not automatically mean that the necessary information will be satisfactorily communicated. For example, the new system of reference notation published in the 11th edition

(UF, BT, RT, SA, NT, and USE) may not be much clearer or more helpful than the older system (X, XX, SA, see also, and see).[18]

Probably nobody would disagree with the first three tenets of the "4 C's" of presentation of data. "Clear," "consistent," and "complete" are always admirable traits in communication. On the other hand, the fourth tenet, "concise," may not find universal concurrence. Yet if presentation of data is not concise, it takes more time to communicate and therefore increases the risk that the message will not be fully or correctly understood. Patience is not one of the most common virtues of modern humanity. In addition, brevity will help save storage space in the computer.

In addition to the "4 C's," it is vital that the data needed to service any heading be presented at the point of primary contact, that is, LC's subject heading listings. Remote guidance is less accessible and therefore less effective. Some elaboration of this tenet is given in principle E5 below.

2. Comprehensive subdivision lists and instructions as to their exact use must be readily available in the LC subject heading system

If subdivisions available for use under primary structural elements are not comprehensively developed and very clearly presented, misunderstanding, confusion, inconsistency of application, and inadequate subject access will typically result. Control of vocabulary, order, and specific function of subdivisions is essential for an effective subject heading system. In recent years, LC has made great strides in the development of a full array of subdivisions and in the explanation of how and when they should be used.[19] Currently, this is one of LC's biggest theoretical strengths, along with the "logical strings" discussed above in B3. (Its outstanding practical asset, probably, is its widespread and long-standing usage throughout the world.) LC should continue their commendable and valuable progress in the area of subdivisions.

3. As much as possible, LC subject headings should be self-explanatory

To the greatest degree which can be practically achieved, LC subject headings should not require additional explanation. As touched upon briefly above in principle C4, scope notes should be avoided if at all possible. Although scope notes have been valuable in the past, there are four problems associated with them. First, they take up a lot of space, and this is a major consideration in online environments. Second, they have been created very inconsistently. Many situations needing scope notes do not have them. Third, they sometimes have established overly restrictive parameters for the subject heading or have established usage inconsistent with similar purpose headings. Fourth, and probably most important, their existence often indicates the presence of a problem of structure or terminology. The resolution of the structural or semantic problem may well result in the deletion of the scope note because there will no longer be any need for any kind of special explanation.

Three examples can demonstrate the difficulties created by problems three and four. In principle C4, the inconsistent definition of the concept of "Philology" was discussed. The scope note under "Classical philology" is as follows:

> Here are entered treatises on the theory, methods and history of classical scholarship.

In contrast, the scope note under "Philology" is as follows:

> Here are entered works dealing with both language and literature. Works limited to language are entered under the heading Language and languages, and those dealing solely with literature, under the heading Literature. Works limited to comparison of grammatical structure are entered under the heading Grammar, Comparative and general.

If, as suggested in C4, the definition of "Philology" was made consistent and a bracketed instruction replaced the scope notes, the inconsistent treatment of the "Philology" concept as well as the confusion between discipline and topic would be eliminated or at least greatly reduced.

A second example of scope note woes is the following paragraph under "Architecture":

> This heading is subdivided by place for works on architecture indigenous to the place named, e.g., Architecture--United States. The heading is qualified by a national qualifier for works on architecture of the type named in the qualifier but located in other places, e.g., Architecture, American--India.

This interpretation of how "Architecture" should be used is at odds with similar purpose headings such as "Art," "Painting," and "Silverwork." If the meaning of "(May Subd Geog)" is broadened and made more flexible and versatile as will be suggested below in E6, and headings of the type "Architecture, American" are abandoned as was suggested above in B5, the scope note under "Architecture" will not be needed. With those two changes, "Architecture," "Art," "Painting," and "Silverwork" subdivided by place will all signify the art genre located in, produced in, and/or in the style of the particular locality. (For example, American style architecture located in India would have the headings "Architecture--United States" and "Architecture--India." We are not used to this type of subject heading psychology, but such patterns provide a remarkable degree of flexibility. It would of course require searching under two headings, but in many other cases, including "Silverwork," the present system requires searching under two or more headings for complex topics. Trying to fully cover complex topics with one heading has created many problematic situations.) With no special definition, treatment, or relationship involved, scope notes would be completely unnecessary.

A third example of scope note problems is "Technology transfer" which has the following explanation under it:

> Subdivided by the region or country receiving the technology. Where applicable, also make an additional entry under this heading with subdivision for the region or country transferring the technology.

The difficulty with this scope note is that it does not provide for works dealing only with the exporting of technology by specific regions or countries. If the function of (May Subd Geog) is broadened as mentioned under the "Architecture" example above,

"Technology transfer" subdivided by place can mean any relationship of technology transfer with the geographical area.

With comprehensive correction of structure, terminology, specificity, and presentation of data throughout LC's main subject heading listing, many scope notes will be rendered unnecessary. For those subject heading situations still requiring some type of explanation after large scale adjustments of structure, terminology, specificity, and presentation of data, succinct and consistent bracketed instructions should serve most if not all of the needs for communication. Elimination of scope notes under the circumstances described will save space overall, provide for a crisper and more patterned presentation of data, and improve the understandability of LC subject headings. These improvements will increase the probability that the harried cataloger and impatient library user will fully comprehend the heading. Scope notes are not very conducive to ready and rapid understanding.

4. "Conditional subjects" should be avoided

An opposing situation to scope notes are "conditional subjects." While scope notes tend to be wordy compensations for problematic structure or terminology, the difficulties of conditional subjects primarily relate to the inadequate communication of subject situations. Perhaps the classic case of "conditional subjects" is the usage of the subdivision "--Law and legislation." Under the heading "Law" the following instruction is offered:

> [use the] subdivision Law and legislation under topics, e.g., Telecommunication--Law and legislation.

This guideline suggests that "--Law and legislation" can be freely used under any topic without restriction. But such is not true. In LC's *Subject Cataloging Manual* the conditions under which "--Law and legislation" cannot be used are spelled out.[20] The subdivision cannot be added after topics for which phrase headings such as "Agricultural laws and legislation" exist, and when the topical heading represents a group of people. In the first case, "--Law and legislation" would be quite redundant, and in the second case the more suitably expressed subdivision "--Legal status, laws, etc." is utilized.

These two exceptions create no major problems. The phrase headings should be changed whenever they can naturally and readily be replaced by two or more shorter structural elements. For example, "Agricultural laws and legislation" would be much better if it were converted to "Agriculture--Law and legislation." In recent years, LC has shown some inclination to make such conversions. The real problem with "--Law and legislation" occurs with a third situation which prohibits use of the subdivision. When, in LC's words, "the topical heading itself is inherently legal, e.g., Torts, Civil procedure, Domestic relations," "--Law and legislation" is not used. But what headings besides the three mentioned are "inherently legal"? Does the average cataloger and library patron really understand enough about law to properly and consistently make such a judgment? Since the "inherently legal" guidelines is vague and allows for much subjective interpretation, the potential for inconsistent application is definitely present. In addition, the "conditional" nature of such headings is not at all indicated in the most important place, where the subject heading is printed in LC's main subject heading listing. As discussed above in E3, subject headings should be self-explanatory as much as possible, and in line with this dictum it is always preferable to have specific instructions printed with a subject heading than to have general instructions located in an external guide and potentially unseen or forgotten. Ideally, a skilled and conscientious cataloger should constantly consult external guides, but in reality such integrity does not always occur.

A solution to this "conditional" situation would be to add the bracketed qualifier "[Legal]" after all headings which cannot be subdivided by "--Law and legislation." The qualifier would not only be added after headings such as "Domestic relations" which are vulnerable to subjective judgments as to whether they are legal, but also after patently "legal" headings such as "Criminal law." The result for these two headings would be:

Domestic relations [Legal]
Criminal law [Legal]

Such modifications may seem to be overkill or at least redundant in some cases, but there will be no doubt as to the status of headings. After this is done, "--Law and legislation" can be converted to a free-floating subdivision under topics, accompanied by an instruction that prohibits its use under any heading with the qualifier "[Legal]."

Bracketed qualifiers have already been established by LC with their development of "[May Subd Geog]" (see E6 below). Bracketed instruction notes have also been proposed by this author in C4 above. So the concept of bracketed qualifiers such as "[Legal]" should fit very well into the scheme of LC subject headings. Perhaps the concept of bracketed qualifiers will spread to other "conditional subject" problems and any other cases where the understandability and/or interpretation of headings would be enhanced by this kind of valuable appendage. Such notation may, in addition, eliminate the need for some scope notes (or the bracketed instruction substitute suggested by this author).

5. Instructions for handling "logical pairs" and similar groupings in LC subject headings must be clearly and comprehensively established

"Logical pairs" are complementary subject headings which must be applied in tandem because of the existence of a two-way or two facet subject relationship. Typical "logical pairs" are:

India--Commerce--China
China--Commerce--India
United States--Relations--Canada
Canada--Relations--United States
French language--Dictionaries--German
German language--Dictionaries--French

"Logical pairs" have been well-developed by LC, and the device is an excellent one. However, the exact specifications for treating "logical pairs" are often not clearly stated although their usage may be inferred from LC's main subject heading listing and other documentation. For example, the indication in the *Subject Cataloging Manual*[21] that the subdivisions "Commerce" and "Relations," which can be used under places, can be further subdivided by place suggests a possible complementary heading in reverse order, but it is far from explicit. LC's *Guide to Subdivision Practice*, on the other hand, does give clear guidance for "Commerce" and the predecessor of "Relations."[22]

To clearly present the necessity for applying a complementary heading in "logical pairs" situations, the following types of instructional notation should be added, wherever needed, in LC's main subject heading listing and other documentation:

> [When subdivided by another place, a reverse order heading is required]
>
> [When subdivided by another language and terms in both languages are given in the terms of the other, a reverse order heading is required but with "language" indicated only in the initial element]

Such notation must be given at the point of primary contact, that is, LC's main subject heading listing, as well as in subdivision lists. External guides such as the *Guide to Subdivision Practice* should not be used as substitutes for having clear instruction at the point of primary contact. After all the subject heading listings are online and universally used in that form, external guides may well be generally ignored. It should be noted that LC has begun to print such instructions in their main subject heading listing. Very helpful notes can be found under "United States--Military relations" and "United States--Relations."

In the case of "Commerce," the first note above would be added in the main subject heading listing under the entry for "Commerce," after the guidance "subdivision Commerce under names of countries, cities, etc." Also, a similar footnote would be added after the entry for "--Commerce" in the list of "Free-floating subdivisions used under names of places." In the case of language dictionaries, the second note above would be added in the main subject heading listing under the entry for "Encyclopedias and dictionaries," after the guidance "subdivision Dictionaries under languages or subjects, e.g., English language--Dictionaries." Also a similar footnote would be added after the entry for "--Dictionaries

--French, [Italian, etc.]" in the list of "Subdivisions controlled by the pattern headings for languages and groups of languages."

The guidelines under the entry for "Encyclopedias and dictionaries" also houses a subject heading with a complementary relationship similar to a "logical pair." When topics are subdivided by "--Dictionaries," for instance, "Botany--Dictionaries," there is always the potential of further subdivision by language, for example, "Botany--Dictionaries--Russian." (If "English" is the language, it is not indicated but instead is implied. This confusing exception should be eliminated!) When the terms of the language indicated in the topical heading are given in the terms of another language, a complementary (but not reverse order) heading is applied, for instance, "Russian language--Dictionaries--Chinese." Another example of complementary headings is the heading "Public opinion." Under that entry is given, among other data, the guidance "and subdivision Foreign public opinion under names of countries, etc." So if the item being cataloged is about the public opinion of persons in the United States relating to the Soviet Union, the following complementary headings are assigned:

Soviet Union--Foreign public opinion, American
Public opinion--United States

To service the complex example of "Botany--Dictionaries--Russian," there could be the notation "[When further subdivided by language and the terms of the language are given in the terms of another language, a complementary heading in the form [language] --Dictionaries--[other language] is required, but with "language" indicated only in the initial element]." Like the examples of "--Commerce" and the other language dictionary situation, the note should be inserted in the appropriate place in LC's main subject heading listing and also as a footnote in the appropriate subdivision list. Granted that this notation and others would be rather lengthy and complex, but the data is needed at the point of primary contact. The addition of specific examples to such notations would greatly enhance the understandability of the notations.

To accommodate the complex example of American public opinion about the Soviet Union would require a very complex notation.

The basic reason for such extra complexity is that the two headings are in reality a circuitous form of a "logical pair." If the interpretation of "(May Subd Geog)" is broadened and made more flexible as suggested above and as elaborated in E6 below, the two headings "Soviet Union--Foreign opinion, American" and "Public opinion --United States" would become "Public opinion--Soviet Union" and "Public opinion--United States," thus eliminating the unnecessary complexity. The two new headings would mean any relationship of public opinion to the two nations. Such a conversion would not only greatly enhance the usage of public opinion subdivided by place and eliminate the need for explanatory notation, but it would in addition put to rest the clumsy inverted subdivision "--Foreign public opinion, British, [French, Italian, etc.]."

The greater the extent that complex complementary relationships are eliminated or simplified by adopting other principles in this volume, the easier it will be for "logical pairs" and similar groupings to be clearly explained at the point of primary contact. In accordance with principle E3 above, which elaborates on the desirability of LC subject headings being as self-explanatory as possible, accommodation of these types of situations and other situations at the point of primary contact will greatly reduce the need for remote elucidation of LC subject headings in external guides.

6. (May Subd Geog) should be eliminated in favor of clearer and more useful notation in LC subject headings

Late in 1986, the meaningless instruction "(Indirect)," which had been source of confusion for users of LC's subject heading system for years, was finally abandoned. It was replaced by the more understandable bracketed instruction "[May Subd Geog]." (Later on, in 1987, LC changed the brackets back to parentheses, but the precedent was retained by the use of brackets around suggested classification numbers in the 11th edition.) Not only was the terminology an improvement, but the initial substitution of brackets for parentheses was an excellent idea. Brackets are superior to parentheses because bracketed notations, which are not part of the subject proper, can be clearly differentiated from parenthetical qualifiers, which are actually part of the subject. By establishing the precedent of using brackets, the way has been opened for the formulation of bracketed instructions, as has been discussed previously.

In spite of the semantic and (for a while) punctuation advances, however, the instruction "(May Subd Geog)" is still identical in function to the old "(Indirect)." The precise interpretation of "(May Subd Geog)" in most subject headings remains unclear and/or debatable. In reality, "(May Subd Geog)" can mean in varying situations "in," "at," "of," "about," "from," "in the style of," "pertaining to," and other terms, plus any combination of terms. Currently, some headings appear to be unrestricted as to their practical usage, for example, "Refugees" which has been implicitly used for refugees *from* an area and also for refugees *in* an area, and "Prisoners of War" which by specific LC instruction can mean prisoners *from* an area and prisoners *in* an area. Other headings, though, are restricted in usage either by specific instruction or by past LC custom. Two examples of specifically restricted headings are the above-mentioned "Technology transfer" which makes no allowance for works dealing only with the exportation of technology from a particular country or region, and "Foreign news," which can only accommodate foreign news *released in* a particular place. Two examples of headings which appear to be restricted by custom are "Diplomats," which tends to mean only diplomats *from* a place, and "Money," which tends to mean only money *in* or *of* a place.

The pervasive inconsistencies and uncertainties associated with the interpretation of "(May Subd Geog)" can be resolved by one fundamental change. If all situations of subdivision by place were allowed to have the greatest possible flexibility and the broadest possible meaning, most inconsistencies, uncertainties, and restrictions in the cataloger's interpretation and usage of such cases would be eliminated. If any and all headings geographically subdivided could mean "in," "at," "of," "about," "from," "pertaining to," "in the style of," etc., or in other words, *anything* relating to the area, the cataloger's handling and understanding of the heading would become so very easy. Complete flexibility and plasticity would replace rigidity and resistance to workability. The four restricted examples above could mean:

Technology transfer [to] and/or [from]
Foreign news [about], [from], and/or [reacted to by]
Diplomats [from] and/or [in]
Money [in], [of], [from], and/or [pertaining to]

In addition, problem headings such as the much discussed "Art, American" could be resolved by broadening the meaning of subdivision by place and by changing "Art, American" to simply "Art." With these improvements, "Art--United States" or "Art--Illinois--Chicago" would mean art located in, produced in, emanating from, and/or in the style of the places as well as other relationships.

Adoption of this concept would certainly make the cataloger's job easier. But will it help the user to better understand LC subject headings and attain a higher degree of subject retrieval? It could be argued that the change would make headings more vague and therefore less effective. However, at present LC in many cases already uses this technique, as discussed above. The proposal is simply to extend a partial LC practice to a blanket LC practice. The alternatives to the concept, moreover, are quite unsatisfactory. The first alternative is to maintain the current inconsistent and confusing situation. The second is to insert a very specific term into every geographically subdivided heading applied. The result would be, for example, "Diplomats [from] China" and "Diplomats [in] France." This would be extremely awkward and perhaps a problem for the computer. The third and equally troublesome alternative is to insert an explanatory note in every situation of geographical subdivision, a most impractical suggestion at the least.

Geographical subdivision is a very complex matter without any ideal solution. The best resolution of the issue is to help both the cataloger and the user by allowing the relationship between topic and place to have the most fluid and broadest function possible. Although specificity in subject headings is normally desirable, in this case it tends to foul up the system. (A semantic note should be made here. "Precision" or "exactness" of subject headings should not be confused with "specificity" or "detail." The former terms imply the degree of match between the topic and the subject heading assigned to express the topic. A heading which is broader than the topic, even considerably broader, is still a match though less so than a heading whose scope is the same as the topic. The latter terms, on the other hand, deal with the degree of narrowness of the subject terms and/or narrowness produced by the usage of subdivisions. A heading could be very detailed or specific and yet be a very poor match with a topic. In contrast, a broad heading like "Science" could be an exact match with a work. Headings with geographical subdivisions, on the other hand, can be potentially very broad, and yet be a perfect match or fit precisely with a work of narrow scope. In this type of case as in the example of the headings separated by slashes discussed above in B9, we have to choose between completely clear and specific headings or a good match. To this author the choice in these situations and all others will always fall strongly on the side of a good match.)

But taking headings subdivided by place to the limits of flexibility and breadth of interpretation may not be enough. It may also be necessary to replace the not highly meaningful parenthetical instruction "(May Subd Geog)" by a more meaningful bracketed instruction such as "[In/of/from]." Even if the interpretation of headings is broadened and their application made much easier, "(May Subd Geog)" does not provide any clear message as to usage. Specific instructions as to the interpretation of "(May Subd Geog)" could be presented in some place(s) external to LC's subject heading listings, and that would be of some help. However, it would be even more helpful if the instruction itself gave significant guidance to the user. Since "[In/of/from]," if liberally viewed, more or less covers the entire spectrum of possibilities, it would be an instruction superior to the bland "(May Subd Geog)." "[In/of/from]" would tend to suggest the wide variety of potential relationship between a topic and a place. But no matter what exact terminology is employed to express the relationship, the expansion of the meaning and usage of subdivision by place is absolutely vital to the continued growth and maturation of the LC subject heading system.

7. "Gathering levels" for concepts should be comprehensively established in the LC subject heading system and be clearly documented

"Gathering levels" is an excellent device for providing additional subject headings which are broader than the main topic involved, so that related topics can be "gathered" or collocated at one point. The term was formulated by LC, and as far as is known, has only been employed in the field of zoology.[23] For example, a book on Illinois robins could have the subjects:

Robins
Birds--Illinois

In this case, "Birds--Illinois" is the gathering level. Using the gathering level technique for this topic eliminates the need to search through countless species of birds to comprehensively access all works on Illinois birds. In addition, it provides a readily understandable secondary access point to the subject. Note that "Robins" was not divided by place because LC's printed and online documentation does not allow it. Although LC now theoretically permits geographical subdivision of biological headings at all levels,[24] at the time of the writing of this book the policy had not been universally transferred into print. However, even if the primary heading were subdivided by place and/or a topical subdivision and thereby fully covered the subject of the book, the gathering level would still be used. The main purpose of the gathering level is not to compensate for the possible incompleteness of the primary heading. Its chief function is to create a broader access point where multiple related items can be brought together to greatly enhance subject retrieval. In such cases, though, it would be much better if all headings had the proper degree of specificity, as discussed above in D1.

Although the terminology "gathering levels" has apparently only been used by LC for zoology, they have explicitly provided gathering levels for some other fields or subject groups, for example, biography, folklore, manuscripts, and vital statistics. It can also be inferred that they may have implicitly or informally utilized gathering levels in botany, geology, and ethnology, and via the subdivisions "--Civilization" and "--Antiquities," as well as in other situations. Some LC records involving individual species of plants have also utilized broad additional headings such as "Trees--[place]." Some LC records involving narrow geological concepts have also utilized broad additional headings such as "Petrology--[place]," "Mineralogy--[place]," or "Geology--[place]." Many

LC records involving a specific ethnic group have also utilized the broader heading "Ethnology--[place]." The heading "[place]--Civilization" has been utilized as a gathering level for topics relating to the psychological, spiritual, mental, and intellectual characteristics of a geographical area. The heading "[place]--Antiquities" has been utilized as a gathering level for the archaeological situation of a geographical area.

This explicit and implicit usage of gathering levels should be officially and openly extended to all areas which can justify the techniques, and in addition all gathering levels should be clearly documented. For example, in LC's main subject heading listing "Mineralogy" could be followed by the bracketed instruction "[Gathering level for individual minerals and groups of minerals]." Also, in LC's lists of subdivisions, "--Antiquities" could be followed by the bracketed instruction "[Gathering level for archaeological findings in a place]." But no matter what the exact method may be for handling gathering levels, their presence must be comprehensively established and readily understood by all.

Ironically, LC recently has proposed discontinuance of this very useful retrieval device. In a 1988 issue of *Cataloging Service Bulletin*, LC stated that they were considering elimination of gathering levels.[25] Supposedly, the reasons for the proposal were to "simplify cataloging" (no justification was given for this statement) and "because their usefulness to catalog users has been questioned." As previously discussed in section B5 and as will be discussed in section A2 and other parts of the chapter on application, a major question continues to arise to challenge this type of thinking. This is, how can anything that eliminates relevant subject headings without effective replacements claim to be in the best interests of the catalog user?

8. Guidelines must be clearly established in the LC subject heading system to determine how to handle cases when a subject is a reflection of the main entry or an added entry

Fairly frequently, one or more subjects assigned may be a reflection of the main entry or an added entry. That is, the main or added entry, whether a person or organization, is the same as or is related to one or more subjects because of a special situation in which the person or organization has complete or partial responsibility for authorship as well as being the topic or part of the topic of the item. Some typical examples are:

autobiography, where a person is the main entry and also a subject (sometimes subdivided);
exhibitions of artists, where the artist is the main entry and also a subject (followed by "--Exhibitions");
biographies of artists, where the artist is a subject and, when the book contains a significant amount of reproductions of the artist's work, also an added entry;
history, personnel, activities, etc., of an organization where the organization is the main entry and also a subject. The organization as a subject may have a form or topical subdivision such as "--Bibliography" or "--History." The organization as a subject may be subdivided by a hierarchical subunit while the main entry is not, or vice versa;
holdings of a library or collections of a museum, where the library or museum is the main entry and also a subject (often with a subdivision such as "--Catalogs").

How to treat the situations described above and all similar cases should be covered by LC in its subject heading documentation. There should be no voids which allow for guesswork by the cataloger and/or user. Since such documentation would be lengthy and complex, it cannot be accomplished directly in LC's subject heading listings. It would have to be presented in an external guide.

9. Guidelines must be clearly established in the LC subject heading system as to when juvenile level headings should be applied

Although LC has used juvenile level headings and subdivisions for many years, there has not been any clear criteria for determining when to use them. Furthermore, the inferences gathered from a review of the occasions when LC has used juvenile level headings and subdivisions support a viewpoint that LC has perhaps misinterpreted their usage. Often, books for groups as old as high school age have been treated as juvenile by LC. It is this author's opinion, however, as well as the opinion of some others, that a much lower threshold should separate juvenile from nonjuvenile material. Certainly by the time the normal student attends American junior high schools, or about age twelve, or about the beginning of puberty, the juvenile label becomes worthless if not insulting. The typical twelve year old is capable of reading many adult level books, and the typical school book for twelve year olds is not well-described by juvenile labels. It is true that age twelve is far from maturity, but at the same time that age and the subsequent several years cannot be adequately served by terms relating to the years of earlier development.

Therefore, age twelve should be the dividing line between juvenile materials and nonjuvenile materials in LC subject heading practice. Materials below that level should receive juvenile treatment, and those at or above that level should not. If some persons are uncomfortable with the placement of the threshold, perhaps the development of "youth" level headings similar to juvenile level headings would take care of this concern. The "youth" level headings could accommodate the period from age twelve through age eighteen. Personally, this author feels that "youth" level headings are not needed and could even make the situation murkier, but they certainly are preferable to using juvenile level headings for ages twelve through eighteen. As low as twelve may seem to some persons, it is actually a compromise position between those who think that age ten or thereabouts should be the threshold and those who believe in a higher dividing line.

10. Terminology used for the presentation of data in the LC subject heading system should be re-evaluated and extensively changed

Throughout the previous part of this volume the inadequacies of the terminology used by LC to describe subject heading situations and phenomena, or the failure to provide terminology, have been apparent on several occasions. It is strongly suggested that LC give serious reconsideration to its subject system vocabulary and change such terminology to more satisfactorily meet present and future needs. For example, LC commonly uses the term "subdivision" to describe a subordinate structural element. But since "subdivision" implies hierarchical arrangement, such as that employed in botanical and zoological classification, a more suitable term to describe the horizontal relationship of subordinate structural elements to the primary structural element would be "subheading."[26] And valid and useful LC terms which have been in the past limited in application, for example, "gathering levels," should be expanded in scope.

Furthermore, LC should consider adopting new terms which describe previously-unverbalized situations, or which describe situations better than in the past. For instance, some of the terminology presented by this author in this volume could be adopted. Terms like "primary structural elements," "subordinate structural elements," "logical strings," "rival headings," "conditional subjects," "reverse patterns," and "logical pairs," which have been discussed above, as well as "primary headings" and "secondary headings" which will be elaborated upon in section B of the following chapter on "Application," should be seriously reviewed with intent to possibly adopt. Even the description of the components of LC's subject heading documentation itself should be re-evaluated. "LCSH" is a freely-used acronym apparently meaning the LC subject heading system, or the two volume "red book" along with its supplements and microfiche and online successors, or both. Rather than throw about this loose and semi-meaningless acronym, more precise terms should be developed and utilized. Throughout this book, an effort has been made to use more exact terminology for the varied documentation of the LC subject heading system. Inclusion of this author's terms or similar precise description into the LC subject heading system will augment and clarify LC's subject heading vocabulary. In case this author's terminology for the components of LC's subject heading documentation has not been clearly understood or closely noticed, the vocabulary is summarized below:

the red books; their supplements; their microfiche and online analogs	=	main subject heading listing
lists of subdivisions no matter where located	=	subdivision lists (or subheading lists)
main subject heading listing plus subdivision lists	=	subject heading listings
any documentation other than the main subject heading listing or the subdivision lists	=	external guides

NOTES

1. Not everybody would agree with this assessment, for example, David Henige. "Library of Congress Subject Headings: Is Euthanasia the Answer?," *Cataloging & Classification Quarterly* 8, no. 1:7-19 (1987). This is a decidedly negative article. The Library of Congress presented a very good response in the same issue.

2. *The Oxford Dictionary of Quotations*. Oxford: Oxford University Press, 1979, p. 150.

3. See *OCLC Annual Report, 1987/88*. Dublin, Ohio: OCLC, 1988, p. 4.

4. See John McKinlay. "Australia, LCSH and FLASH." *Library Resources and Technical Services*, 26:107 (April/June 1982). He makes a very strong statement about LC's responsibilities to the rest of the world.

5. They are all located in the *Subject Cataloging Manual: Subject Headings*. Rev. ed. Washington, D.C.: Library of Congress, 1985.

6. The proposal was made in *Cataloging Service Bulletin* 35: 37-38 (Winter 1987); the withdrawal of the proposal was in *Cataloging Service Bulletin* 38: 71-72 (Fall 1987). A rebuttal to the first item above can be found in Studwell, William E. "A Structural Step Backward?", *RTSD Newsletter* 12:28-29 (Summer 1987).

7. *Subject Cataloging Manual*, section H830.

8. *Subject Cataloging Manual*, section H1152.

9. *Subject Cataloging Manual*, section H832.

10. The *Subject Cataloging Manual*, section H1140, indicates that "--Public buildings" is no longer a valid subdivision under places.

11. Martine Blanc-Montmayer, and Françoise Danset. *Choix de vedettes materières à l'intention des bibliothèques*. Nouv. Éd. Paris: Cercle de la librairie, 1987, p. xxiv. Note that only the basic slash concept was given here. The extension of the concept is this author's.

12. *Cataloging Service Bulletin* 40:46 (Spring 1988).

13. *Cataloging Service Bulletin* 39:27 (Winter 1988).

14 Section H1149 of the *Subject Cataloging Manual* deals with subdivisions under chemicals but not name forms of chemicals.

15. Marcia J. Bates. "Rethinking Authority Control for Online Catalog Subject Access." (unpublished paper, 1988). This two page document for an online superthesaurus of see references merits consideration by LC.

16. *Subject Cataloging Manual*, section H1647.

17. *Subject Cataloging Manual*, section H1155.2.

18. See Mary Dykstra. "LC Subject Headings Disguised as a Thesaurus," *Library Journal* 113, no. 4:42-46 (March 1, 1988). Primarily, this is a commentary on the new codes for references developed by LC.

19. Subdivisions and their usage are well documented in the *Subject Cataloging Manual*.

20. *Subject Cataloging Manual*, section H1705.

21. *Subject Cataloging Manual*, section H1140, p. 2 and 5.

22. *Library of Congress Subject Headings: A Guide to Subdivision Practice*. Washington: Library of Congress, 1981, p. 30 and 61. Note that this valuable guide is now somewhat obsolete.

23. *Cataloging Service* 122:16-18 (Summer 1977); the concept of gathering levels in biology was later published in the *Subject Cataloging Manual*, section H1332, but without using the term "gathering levels" or really explicitly stating that gathering levels should be employed.

24. *Cataloging Service Bulletin* 41:84 (Summer 1988).

25. *Cataloging Service Bulletin* 41:83-84 (Summer 1988).

26. Proposed in William E. Studwell and Paule Rolland-Thomas. "The Form and Structure of a Subject Heading Code," *Library Resources and Technical Services* 32:168 (April 1988).

Chapter 2

Application: Philosophy and Problems

The principles set forth in the above chapter apply to the structure of, terminology of, specificity in, presentation of data for, and the overall nature of the Library of Congress subject heading system. But the establishment of principles for the system itself must be supplemented by principles which aid in the everyday practice of interpreting and applying LC subject headings. Even with a sound, logical, consistent, and easily understood subject heading system, some guidelines for interpreting the system are needed. Accordingly, fifteen principles relating to practice are elaborated below. As in the previous chapter, there is no claim that these principles comprise the total potential knowledge on the topic.

PRINCIPLES RELATING TO THE APPLICATION OR INTERPRETATION OF LIBRARY OF CONGRESS SUBJECT HEADINGS

A. General

1. Subject cataloging is an art

Good subject cataloging requires a substantial knowledge of the subject cataloging system and sufficient knowledge of the topics being cataloged. A good subject cataloging system, furthermore, is based on scientific and logical principles. Yet the salient characteristic of subject cataloging is neither of these very important factors, but instead the concept that subject cataloging is definitely an art.

All of cataloging is to some degree an art, but subject cataloging is perhaps more dependent on the judgment and skill of the cataloger than are descriptive cataloging and classification. All subject catalogers have access to the same subject heading documentation, but the results of subject cataloging vary widely from cataloger to cataloger. Part of the variance is training and the environment of quality surrounding each cataloger, but the combination of experience, education, and ability which each cataloger brings to the task of subject cataloging is the main determinant of the subject cataloging product.

This dominant characteristic of subject cataloging must not be undervalued or forgotten. No matter how solid a foundation a subject cataloging system may possess, its implementation is always at the mercy of the interpretation of the subject cataloger. To deny this premise is to deny that there are variances in skill and effectiveness of physicians, carpenters, engineers, cooks, police detectives, reference librarians, gardeners, managers, etc. So although the LC subject heading system is an effective one, and potentially more effective after adopting those principles and concepts in the previous chapter which are new to their system, the overall long-term success of subject cataloging using the LC system is dependent on the art of the individual subject cataloger. Thoroughly understanding this vulnerability of the LC system will, as with all systems, help strengthen its application by increased sensitivity, care, and dedication to producing satisfactory subject access. Ignoring this pervasive feature of the system, or in other words, believing that a good subject heading system by itself will result in good subject access, will tend to undermine the goals and purposes of the system.

2. It cannot be presumed that the subject cataloger understands perfectly, or that the user of subject cataloging understands perfectly

Subject cataloging is a means of communication, and a subjective one. The subjectivity, furthermore, exists at both ends of the subject access process. It never can be presumed that the producer of subject headings, the cataloger, or the consumer of subject headings, the library user, understands thoroughly, clearly, or perfectly the subject situation for any particular item. This is not to say that a certain degree of competence is not present at both ends of the process. Rather, it is a realization that humans control all aspects of subject cataloging, and that to expect consistently perfect execution on the part of the subject cataloger, no matter how skilled, or perfect understanding on the part of the library user, no matter how intelligent, would be folly. Even with the best subject heading system, this delicate condition would still be a significant factor.

So to place the success of subject retrieval solely on one subject heading is potentially risky. There are of course many circumstances where the subject situation is comparatively obvious, apparent, or easy to comprehend and therefore one heading would normally serve well. A general history of France, a textbook of general physics, an introduction to plane geometry, and a world atlas are examples of subjects which will probably be well understood and well-covered by a single subject heading. And collections of an individual's poems, individual plays and novels, and similar phenomena which by LC practice normally do not receive any subject at all usually are not a problem. But when there are potential multiple subjects, potential multiple aspects to a subject, and/or any significant degree of subject complexity, the risk of unsatisfactory subject access increases. To cover such circumstances, which are probably a majority of subject situations, multiple subjects are needed. LC, which in the relatively distant past tended to be very frugal with its subject headings, has in recent years applied multiple headings on more and more occasions and has generally increased the number of headings on cataloging records. This trend is a clear sign that they recognize the importance of increased access points.

With the broader array of potential access provided by multiple headings, the potential consequences of the imperfections of either the subject cataloger or the library user are diminished. Presuming a reasonable degree of competence at both ends, the larger the number of subjects applied tends to mean the smaller the risk of unsatisfactory subject access. Or, stated in another way, there is a direct correlation between the amount of competent and relevant headings applied and the chance for effective subject retrieval. This semi-axiom, however, is not absolute. There are simply too many intangibles. And the premise can definitely be carried too far. But it has been this author's observation that as a whole supplying an expanded number of headings, within reasonable quantitative limits, and putting them in some semblance of logical order, will provide considerable more potential for subject retrieval than the alternatives. This proposition will be elaborated upon in the next three sections, "Secondary Headings," "Number of Subjects," and "Order of Subjects."

B. "Secondary Headings"

1. "Secondary headings" should be extensively utilized in the application of LC subject headings

As discussed above, increasing the quantity of subject headings has a tendency to increase the effectiveness of subject access. But this understanding by itself does not make the subject cataloger fully knowledgeable in the handling of multiple subject headings. Two other elements are required. The first is a better set of terms to describe the two basic types of subject headings. LC in a way recognizes that there are two type of headings in the matter of intent or purpose. When they use only one heading, it is called a "uniform heading." When they use more than one heading, the second and subsequent headings are called "duplicate entries."[1] These terms, though, are not really meaningful. If, for example, the logical pair "United States--Foreign relations--France" and "France--Foreign relations--United States" is applied, LC would call the first heading a "uniform heading" and the second a "duplicate entry." And if, for example they use "Gnatcatchers" plus "Birds--California," LC would again call the first heading a "uniform heading" and the second a "duplicate entry." In the first example, however, the two headings have the same purpose, but are just reversed in order. In the second example, the two headings have distinctly different purposes. So to describe these two dissimilar pairs with identical terms is not really helpful.

Instead, this author's terms "primary" and "secondary," should be substituted for LC's ineffective descriptors. "Primary headings" are those which reflect the principal or dominant theme or themes. A book entirely on the history of Chicago would have one primary subject, "Chicago (Ill.)--History." A textbook of calculus and analytical geometry would have two primary headings, "Calculus" and "Geometry, Analytic." In contrast, "secondary headings" are those which reflect a concept or topic which is in some way less essential for subject access than primary headings but which is still desirable for optimal subject retrieval. A book on entrepreneurship in Taiwan could have the primary heading "Entrepreneurship--Taiwan" and the secondary heading "Taiwan--Economic conditions." Without the secondary heading in this case, there would definitely be less potential for access. In reality, this particular secondary heading is almost as important for retrieval as the primary heading.

Applying the descriptors "primary" and "secondary" to the two pairs of headings touched upon earlier, both of the headings "United States--Foreign relations--France" and "France--Foreign relations--United States" would be primary headings. They both have the same basic roles, functions, or purposes. They both express the dominant theme of the material being cataloged. But the headings "Gnatcatchers" and "Birds--California" do not have the same roles, functions, or purposes. "Gnatcatchers," which reflects the fundamental theme of the material being cataloged, is a primary heading. "Birds--California," which is another broader way to access the gnatcatchers of California, is a secondary heading. It is, as discussed above, a "gathering level." So is "Taiwan--Economic conditions."

Whether or not primary headings such as "Gnatcatchers" and "Entrepreneurship" can be subdivided by place, secondary headings such as the ones given in the above examples should be consistently applied. Although the primary headings if augmented by place might express the theme of the item perfectly, the secondary headings would still be needed because of the principle of "gathering levels."

All secondary headings, however, are not gathering levels. Since gathering levels reflect only the main topic(s) by presenting it in a different way or employing a different emphasis or dealing with a different facet, nondominant themes do not fall under the umbrella of gathering levels. If significant, though, nondominant topics must be accessed. For instance, if the item on gnatcatchers also had some emphasis on the insects of California, another secondary heading,

"Insects--California," would be applied. And for instance, if the item on entrepreneurship also dealt significantly with the politics of Taiwan, another secondary heading, "Taiwan--Politics and government" would be applied. Both of these additional secondary headings do not function as gathering levels (although in other cases they might be) but instead cover nondominant themes.

The second element required to effectively handle multiple subject headings is a better understanding as to their use. In the above elaboration on the employment of "primary" and "secondary" to describe the two functional types of headings, there were some examples as to how and when to use secondary headings. If in their subject heading documentation, external to the subject heading listings, LC provided an extensive guide to the differences between primary and secondary headings, and the usage of secondary headings including general guidelines on gathering levels, it would greatly aid in the comprehension of subject heading application. As part of the elucidation on secondary headings, it should be made abundantly clear that secondary headings, whether of the gathering level type or of the nondominant theme type, are encouraged by LC. It is not sufficient to explain how certain types of headings should be handled. It is also essential that the extent of usage be readily understood. (Most users, however, will not be really concerned with understanding about the different types of headings and their usage, but instead how effective retrieval is. Display of the full array of subjects on the online catalog screen [see the chapter on "The Future"] may be quite helpful to the user, though.) In addition, the Library of Congress staff should make more liberal their view on secondary headings. In recent years, they have definitely increased the number of secondary headings on cataloging records. This very favorable trend should continue and even be more expanded.

There are, of course, limits to which secondary headings should be utilized. Establishing a standard for the maximum allowable number of subjects, as proposed in C3 below, will help considerably in controlling abuse of secondary heading application. Adoption of principle B2 below will also aid in controlling number and relevancy. Overall, although encouraging the greater use of secondary headings has some potential for misuse, assigning a more extensive amount of secondary headings provides much more potential for access. Furthermore, with the increasing presence of online catalogs the economic objections of having to prepare and file too many catalog cards will increasingly become less valid.

2. Policies should be established by LC to cover the entire range of topics to which secondary headings frequently apply

In conjunction with the above-described documentation on the usage of secondary headings, LC should develop and promulgate specific policies to cover the spectrum of subject situations to which secondary headings frequently or commonly apply. This documentation should be presented external to LC's subject heading listings and would complement this author's proposed insertion of bracketed instructions for gathering levels directly in LC's subject heading listings. LC has already provided detailed policies for some areas, for example, zoology, biography, folklore, and manuscripts.[2] In all such cases, the options for applying gathering level type secondary headings are clearly delineated. The fine work done for these categories should be extended as comprehensively as possible through the LC subject heading system. When that is accomplished, LC will have produced one of the most valuable policy packages since the inception of LC subject headings.

In addition to increasing potential retrieval by increasing the usage of secondary headings, the development of such policies will tend to control the number and relevancy of secondary headings by clearly suggesting patterns to be followed in all the situations. The implementation of those policies already produced by LC, for instance, the detailed elucidation of secondary headings for biography, has resulted in better-controlled arrays of subjects. In the case of biographies, patterns such as the following are allowed and encouraged:

[person]
Generals--United States--Biography
United States. Army--Biography
World War, 1939-1945--France

There has been some debate as to the retrieval value of such patterns. Since headings two and three serve as gathering levels, the argument for their usefulness is covered by the discussion on gathering levels. The fourth heading, however, is different from the second and third. The main purpose of that heading is not to access a biography, but to cover other aspects of the item being cataloged. It could be a gathering level or it could be a heading covering a nondominant theme. In either case it is a useful access point. Together, the set of four headings should be an effective quartet for the retrieval of the person and important subthemes.

The result of this type of pattern are orderly, systematic, and useful arrays of headings. When secondary headings are well-controlled in vocabulary and in relationship like in this situation, the potential for good subject access is increased. That is where the control of secondary headings should primarily be focused. The quantity of subjects is certainly a concern, but one which can be fairly easily alleviated. The vocabulary and relationship of secondary headings, that is, which headings and in which order, are on the other hand a much more important matter. One suspects that part of the reason for controlling the number of headings in the past may have been, even unconsciously, the lack of established policies for the choice and order of secondary headings in subject situations. With the development of a comprehensive set of policies as is proposed here, many more cataloging records will have much better subject access because of the twin advantages of more subjects and better-controlled subject arrays. (More about the importance of proper order of subjects will be given in D below.)

3. When the main theme focuses substantially on a specific geographical area, an effort should be made to assure that the place is the primary structural element in at least one LC subject heading, and/or that at least one gathering level subdivided by place is used

Access by place is an important aspect of retrieval in the LC subject heading system. When a specific geographical area is significantly associated with the dominant theme of the item being cataloged, access by place should be provided if at all reasonable.

There are two different ways such coverage can be accomplished. One is by assigning at least one gathering level type heading subdivided by place. For example, the study of a specific ethnic group in Indonesia would have the following subjects:

> [ethnic group]
> Ethnology--Indonesia

Also, the history of a French railroad line would have the following subjects:

> [name of railroad line]--History
> Railroads--France--History

Currently, these types of situations are frequently well-covered by LC in their cataloging records. If such practices are comprehensively applied, as proposed above in the principle on gathering levels, this method will become automatic.

Method number two is to assign a heading beginning with the geographical area needing retrieval. For example, the history of a Chinese gentlemen's club in Singapore could have the following subjects:

> [name of club]--History
> Chinese--Singapore--History
> Singapore--History

"Singapore--History," which is a completely relevant secondary heading in this case because various aspects of Singapore's history are being covered, will take care of the need for direct access by place. Both "Singapore--History" and "Chinese--Singapore--History" are, in addition, gathering levels. So the subject of this item would be well accommodated by the combination of the gathering levels plus the place as the primary or initial structural element. Currently, this type of situation also is frequently well-covered by LC.

Another example of method two is its application to maps. If maps depicting the geology of Italy and transportation in Japan are being cataloged, the following subjects could be assigned:

Geology--Italy--Maps
Italy--Maps
Transportation--Japan--Maps
Japan--Maps

It could be argued that because "Geology" and "Transportation" are in actuality gathering levels, the added gathering level subjects accessing the places directly are not needed. But in addition to the reasons given in the Singapore situation above, maps, which are so intimately intertwined with geographical areas, should have automatic provision of subjects beginning with place. Furthermore, the assignment of the added subjects follows the general psychology of good secondary subject application. So whether the gathering level method and/or the place as the initial element method is used, provision for ready access by place is vital in all cases when a geographical area is a substantial focus of the item being cataloged.

4. In assigning LC subject headings, multiple minor topics should be covered by one or more subjects, if at all feasible, in addition to the major, dominant, or strongly emphasized topic(s)

A fair amount of materials to be cataloged are multi-theme works. Some of such publications contain multiple topics of roughly parallel emphasis, for example, two fields of mathematics, three biographies, and the history of two places. Other multi-theme works, however, have a different setup. These could be described as "major + minor" subject relationships and "minor + major" subject relationships. A "major + minor" situation exists when there are one or more subjects which are major, dominant, or strongly emphasized, along with multiple minor or less emphasized topics. A "minor + major" situation exists when there is no major, dominant, or strongly emphasized topic, but there is a somewhat emphasized theme present. (Multiple minor theme works which can be covered by one to three subjects, such as ten Russian biographies, fifteen fish species or an assortment of topics falling under the discipline of economics, are not to be confused with "major + minor" or "minor + major." Such multiple minor theme works are usually relatively easy to handle.)

"Minor + major" will be discussed in the next principle. This principle deals with "major + minor" situations. One example of a "major + minor" relationship is a work on the civilization of India which also deals in small amounts with the politics, economics, social conditions, religion, and geography of the country. The major theme would of course be covered by the subject "India --Civilization." In this case, the several minor topics will be adequately covered by a secondary heading for the country without subdivision, that is, just "India." Extending this example into a more complex environment, the work in addition could to some extent be about the geology, plant life, and animal life of the country. For this situation three subjects would work out well:

India--Civilization
Natural history--India
India

The heading "Natural history--India" would accommodate the geology, botany, and zoology of the nation, which are nondominant yet collectively of some importance. The broad but not useless heading "India" will serve as an umbrella for all the remaining bits and pieces relating to the country.

All "major + minor" situations, though, are not as homogeneous as the two India cases which in spite of multiple topics all revolve around India. There are some "major + minor" situations in which the minor elements are not closely connected with the major theme(s), or are even totally irrelevant. Again returning to India, a work predominantly on the civilization of India yet with recurrent allusions to Chinese art, music, theater, and literature (not in India but in China itself) could be covered by:

India--Civilization
Arts--China

The examples that could be given for "major + minor" situations are numerous. The key factors in "major + minor" cases are to recognize the pattern and to apply headings according to the guidelines suggested above.

5. In assigning LC subject headings for works which contain no major, dominant, or strongly emphasized topic(s), and which can be accommodated by one or two subjects covering the multiple minor topics, consideration should be given to adding a heading for any somewhat emphasized topic which may be present

This principle deals with the "minor + major" relationship mentioned and defined in the previous principle. The prime characteristic of "minor + major" is the assignment of the single most emphasized theme as a secondary heading because the primary heading collectively represents multiple lesser concepts effectively tied together by one heading. Once again returning to the land of Gandhi and Hinduism, a work on many aspects of India but having a fair amount of emphasis (yet not dominant) on the civilization of the country would have the headings:

India
India--Civilization

In the same spirit, a work on multiple aspects of botany but with a clear yet nondominant thread of ecological themes interspersed throughout would be effectively accessed by the two headings:

Botany
Botany--Ecology

In "minor + major" relationships, as in "major + minor" situations, every case is not homogeneous. There are works which have multiple affiliated minor topics but which also include a subtheme that is considerably different or atypical. For example, if a work having a variety of minor topics which are well accommodated by the heading "Archaeology" also contains frequent references to phenomena and discoveries in the field of astronomy, a second subject "Astronomy" would be applied.

As in the "major + minor" relationship, there are two key considerations in dealing with "minor + major." The first is the recognition of the pattern, and the second is the application of headings following the guidelines suggested above.

C. Number of Subjects

1. In assigning LC subject headings, the maximum number of different persons or places or organizations which can be used for any individual cataloging record should normally be six

The quantity of headings to be assigned to a single cataloging record is not always an easy decision. LC has not provided any clear guidelines for many if not most of the situations in which multiple headings are required. In recent years LC has supplied more headings on the average than in earlier times, and therefore has given us in practice some indication of what quantitative limits there should be.

For situations where multiple persons, or places, or organizations are treated in one work, LC has not explicitly issued any policy. One policy which could be construed as applying to persons, places, and organizations is the instruction to its subject catalogers, "Assign a broad or generic heading that encompasses all the topics treated in a work covering four or more topics."[3] However, in a strict sense, persons, places, and organizations are not topics, but instead are actually entities. LC has in various ways recognized the difference between topics and the entity status of persons, places, and organizations, for instance, in MARC tagging and their preparation of subdivision lists. Therefore it can reasonably be presumed that the "four or more topic" dictum does not apply to entities. Furthermore, no other known LC policy has any relevance to the matter of persons, places, and organizations.

Recent Library of Congress practice, on the other hand, has provided some guidance. Based on LC cataloging which assigns four, five, six or even more persons, places, or organizations to one record, and on the perceptions of this author, a standard of six is proposed. That is, up to six different persons, or six different places as initial elements, or six different organizations can be used on one cataloging record. If more than six persons, or places, or organizations are treated in the work being cataloged, the multiple persons, places, or organizations should be collectively accommodated by one or more broad headings. And in every case when headings have been assigned for individual persons, individual places, or individual organizations, additional pertinent secondary headings should be applied. Even if the proposed maximum of six has been utilized, one or two secondary headings covering a collective concept or two will provide better potential subject access.

One thing that should be remembered here is that this is a guideline, not an absolute. If there are strong reasons for more headings, the cataloger should use his/her discretion and add more headings. The old worries about too many headings in the catalog card environment will most likely dissipate or even disappear in an online environment.

2. In assigning LC subject headings, the maximum number of uses of the same person, place, organization, or topic on any individual cataloging record should be three

Just as there should be a maximum standard for the number of different persons, places, or organizations on one cataloging record, there should also be an explicitly stated maximum for the number of times the same personal name, place name as an initial element, organizational name, or topic can be used on an individual cataloging record. Based on perceived trends in recent LC cataloging, plus the viewpoint of this author, a standard of three is proposed. That is, a person, a place as initial element, an organization, or a topic cannot be repeated more than twice. If the material being cataloged dictates more than three uses, the person, place, organization, or topic should be used only once, and without subdivision. Two examples using the "India" and "Botany" illustrations given in B5 above are:

A) India--Civilization
India--Social conditions
India--Economic conditions
(If the material contains significant additional aspects about India, enough to justify another heading beginning with "In-

dia," just one broad heading for "India" without subdivision should be used.)

B) Botany--Anatomy
Botany--Embryology
Botany--Ecology
(If the material contains significant additional aspects of botany, enough to justify another heading beginning with "Botany" or "Botanical," just one broad heading for "Botany" without subdivision should be used. Note that headings which have the same basic purpose but which because of irregular structure, inversion, or even valid reasons such as semantics have a different form, should be treated in a similar manner. Therefore "Botany--[Subdivision]," "Botanical [other word]," and related configurations of the same subject field should be regarded as falling under the same standard of three. The standard should not just apply to literally identical patterns, but to any patterns having the same fundamental intent.) Again it should be noted that this numerical standard is a guideline, not an absolute.

3. In assigning LC subject headings, the total number of subjects on any individual cataloging record should normally not exceed six, with eight allowed in special cases

In principle C1 above, it was suggested that up to eight subject headings could be allowed under certain circumstances. Normally, though, six should be the total number of subjects on one cataloging record. This proposed standard is, once again, based on a combination of recent LC practice[4] and this author's perceptions. In situations such as the one mentioned in C1 where the proposed maximum of six persons, places, or organizations has been applied, up to two additional secondary headings are encouraged. Therefore in these special cases, eight should be the maximum. But in all other situations, the application of more than six headings should normally be prohibited. Once again, the standard of six should not be absolute, or set in stone, for there may well be some cases where more than six would be desirable. As a whole, however, six should be the upper quantitative limit with the exception of the C1 type situation.

D. Order of Subjects

1. In assigning LC subject headings, the order of subjects is important, with the first subject reflecting the classification and vice versa

In addition to determining what the subjects should be, and how to exactly verbalize the subjects using LC's subject terms and subdivisions, it is also vital that the order of the subjects given represent the order of importance of the concepts involved. (This presumes that the entire array of subjects is available to the user. The advantages of the full display of subjects will be discussed in detail in the chapter on "The Future.") Properly constructed subject headings faithfully portraying the content of the material being cataloged are somewhat sabotaged if a thoughtful effort to correctly put the subjects in order is not made. It is true that choice of order is as subjective as choice of headings, but the more truly representative the cataloger can make the sequence of headings, the more valuable the array of headings becomes. In most cases, there is a big difference in the degree of emphasis between the first subject and the third, fourth, fifth, or sixth subjects when the array of headings are properly ordered. If the subjects are of parallel importance, for instance, four biographies, then obviously the order of the four personal names is not essential. However, the position of secondary headings in such cases, for example, "[topic]--Biography" or "[place]--Biography," is not a trivial matter. For four biographies, the gathering level(s) should be given first, followed by the four personal names. This order makes sense because the principal theme of the material being cataloged is collective biography, not the first personal name to appear in the list of subjects applied. This has not been common practice in the past, but this concept should be fully adopted to make the array of headings more accurately ordered.

When subjects are carefully put in the proper order, descending from most important to least important, some very useful information is provided to the user. This helpful data could be described as the "composite subject picture." Not only are the subjects indicated by the choice of headings, but they are also given a value. The degree of emphasis, the relative significance, and the quantity of space allotted are at least somewhat suggested by the order. If the user knows that the order has meaning, except for obvious cases of parallelism, it will help the user choose which cataloging records are of the greatest utility. Certainly an item with the searched-for subject in the dominant first spot would normally be preferred over an item with the searched-for subject in the fourth or sixth spot. Part of the education of the user must focus on the significance of subject heading order. Otherwise, the array of subjects loses some of its message. Unfortunately, some online catalogs may not necessarily list headings in the order created by the cataloger. Since order of headings can imply a value to each heading, the randomness of such online listing somewhat reduces the effectiveness of the headings. While the online environment makes the choice of main entry less vital, the same does not really apply to subject heading order.

Furthermore, the first subject should reflect the classification assigned and vice versa. The term "reflect" in this context means to directly and strongly relate to each other. In some cases, the first subject and classification clearly match. In other cases, they do not exactly match but instead in some way definitely relate to each other. Therefore, "reflect" rather than "match" is a more meaningful and accurate choice of terminology. If the classification and the first subject do not reflect each other, one or the other was incorrectly chosen and some adjustment is required.

With the exception of the type of situation portrayed by the "four biographies" case elaborated above, LC generally has tended to follow the "order is important" dictum. LC should more fully follow this principle, plus adopt the concept presented in the "four biographies" case, and explicitly incorporate the principle and the concept into their body of subject policy. LC also has tended to follow the "first subject reflects the classification and vice versa" concept, but again should completely abide by it and document it in their policy.

2. In assigning LC subject headings, the first subject should represent the basic purpose of the item being cataloged, or the thing really affected

In the above principle, the advantages of having the first subject truly represent the dominant theme were stated. The dominant theme is not always a single entity. As has been shown by the "four biographies" situation above and by "minor + major" relationships, the dominant theme can be a collective phenomenon. But whether the dominant theme is singular or collective, the first subject should represent the fundamental purpose, the thing really affected, or the essential reason for being. For example, a work on surgery for nurses, in which the principles of surgical knowledge and techniques are explained in a manner particularly suitable for the nursing profession, should have surgery as the first subject and nursing as the second. The basic purpose is for nurses to better understand the field of surgery and not to prepare them to assist in surgery. On the other hand, a work on surgical nursing, which directly provides nurses with the information needed to prepare them to be surgical nurses, should have surgical nursing as the first subject, plus any other pertinent topics. In both cases, nurses would be able to readily access the work since subjects related to nursing would be available on both records. It would be misleading, though, to establish a nursing heading as the first subject just because nurses are the most likely clientele. Establishing headings based on expected audience rather than on actual content is fallacious. A guidebook on travel in the United States which is written in Japanese, for instance, is intended for a Japanese audience. Yet no heading for Japan or Japanese would be applied.

It is not always easy to determine the basic purpose or the thing really affected. For instance, a work on cancer development in the lungs of a laboratory rat is not about the rat, but about lung cancer. The rat is merely the instrument or medium. And sometimes the allotment of space in a work can be misleading. A theme taking up the majority of space in a work can be only the prelude or an adjunct to the fundamental purpose. The prelude or adjunct should of course be accommodated by a secondary heading, and therefore be quite accessible, but the thing really affected or the true reason for being has to be the first heading. Otherwise, the array of subjects would be misleading because of poor ordering. Likewise, the classification, if faithfully reflecting and reflected by the first subject, would not be the best choice.

E. Parallelism of Subjects

1. In assigning LC subject headings, multiple similar purpose subjects of similar importance should receive parallel treatment

"Parallelism" in subject cataloging is the philosophy that similar purpose subjects of roughly equal importance or emphasis should be treated in a parallel or like manner. For instance, for a work with six biographical sketches in which the space allotted to and/or emphasis on each person is somewhat the same, the parallelism principle dictates that all six persons be assigned as individual subjects. However, if one person is definitely emphasized, with the other five being subordinate in the work, only the highly emphasized person is assigned as an individual subject with one or more collective subjects such as "[topic or place]--Biography" assigned to take care of the five lesser emphasized persons. Again the parallelism principle applies. The five lesser emphasized persons have parallel emphasis in the work, and therefore receive parallel treatment by not being assigned as individual subjects. If in this case, the cataloger chose to assign two or three personal names as subjects, the parallelism principle would be violated.

Another example of parallelism is the situation of a work on human physiology which describes the effect of several chemical compounds on the brain. In addition to subjects for the brain and for physiological chemistry as a collective concept, parallelism would dictate that unless one or more chemical compounds are clearly emphasized, all or none of the several compounds should be given as individual subjects. Presuming roughly equal emphasis, all of the compounds would be subjects if there is sufficient material about the compounds, that is, if the compounds are not of tertiary importance, and if the number of headings does not exceed the quantitative standards explained above in C3. If either the quantitative standard is exceeded or the amount of attention given to each compound is slight, none of the compounds would be subjects.

Parallelism, which should not be confused with the decision to use secondary headings, is simply a matter of common sense combined with a desire to assign subjects in an even-handed manner. As logical as parallelism is, it is frequently not adhered to in assigning subject headings. Parallelism should be a constant dictum for the subject cataloger.

2. In assigning LC subject headings, subdivisions should receive parallel treatment if appropriate

Just as the subjects assigned should follow the parallelism principle the subdivisions added to subjects should also be parallel if applicable. Presuming the presence of parallelism, there are only two caveats pertaining to parallel subdivisions. First, the particular subdivision lists being used must allow the use of parallelism. For example, if a work contains the biographies of three literary authors, the names of all three authors would be subdivided by "--Biography" since the list of subdivisions for literary authors permits the subdivision "--Biography." Parallelism flourishes in this situation. Likewise, a work on five persons in public life would result in parallel subdivision treatment since the list of subdivisions for persons other than literary authors does not allow the subdivision "--Biography." Therefore, none of the names of the five persons would be so subdivided. On the other hand, if a work contains the biographies of two literary authors and three other persons, parallelism could not occur. The two literary authors would receive the subdivision "--Biography" but the three persons not literary authors would have no such subdivision. This quirk suggests that some adjustment to these two lists may be in order.

Second, if irregular elements are involved in subject cataloging, full subdivision parallelism might not be applied. For example, if a work is a catalog of a museum's holdings of American paintings depicting women, there would be three subjects:

Painting, American--Catalogs
Women in art--Catalogs
[museum]--Catalogs

The subdivision "--Catalogs" applies to all three subjects, and is allowed by the pertinent subdivision lists, and therefore parallelism dictates the use of the subdivision after all three subjects.

Also, if a work is on the history of a certain petroleum company in Oklahoma, with an appreciable amount of material on the overall history of the state, the subjects might be:

[Company]--History
Petroleum industry and trade--Oklahoma--History
Oklahoma--History

The subdivision "--History" applies to all three subjects, and is allowed by the pertinent subdivision lists, and therefore parallelism dictates the use of the subdivision after all three subjects.

In addition, if a work contains the papers of a conference on English language American literature, English language Canadian literature, and the overall cultures of the two countries, the subjects would be:

American literature--History and criticism--Congresses
Canadian literature--History and criticism--Congresses
United States--Civilization--Congresses
Canada--Civilization--Congresses

The subdivision "--Congresses" applies to all four subjects, and the use of the subdivision is allowed, and therefore parallelism dictates the use of the subdivision after all four subjects.

However, if one or more irregular elements exists in the above situations, parallelism would not be applied to all subjects. In the "--Catalogs" example, if there was a significant section of the teaching of painting in the United States, another heading, "Painting--Study and teaching--United States," would be added, and parallelism would not apply. In the "--History" example, if there was a significant section outlining the personal and business ethics of the company's founder, another heading, "Ethics," would be added, and parallelism would not apply. In the "--Congresses" example, if the work was a festschrift with sufficient material on the person being honored, the name of the honored person would be a subject, but without subdivision. Parallelism again would not apply.

In many if not most cases where parallelism exists, full subdivision parallelism would apply. When parallelism is not present in the array of subject headings, subdivision parallelism is not an issue.

3. In assigning LC subject headings, the use of secondary headings should be as parallel as possible within the same discipline, and as parallel as possible between different disciplines

This principle again is a matter of simple logic. To help attain as even-handed and consistent application of subject headings as is possible, the use of secondary headings should reflect parallelism to the greatest extent. Why does LC, for example, typically use "Silverwork" and "Furniture" as secondary headings for reproductions of the work of individual artists in these two genres, but not "Painting" or "Sculpture" for reproductions of the work of individual artists in those genres? On a theoretical basis, such secondary headings should be parallel, that is, secondary headings should be used in all or none of these similar situations. Since secondary headings are to be encouraged, the preference is that secondary headings be used in all cases. For art genres, LC apparently has followed the implicit policy that the major fields of art should not have secondary headings of this type, most likely to reduce the large amount of headings under these broad categories. This practical approach to the discipline of art by LC does have considerable justification. But if LC wants to continue this policy of exception to parallel treatment within the discipline, it should explicitly and clearly document the exception.

Maximal parallelism in the use of secondary headings should not just be a strong element in the discipline of art, but in all other disciplines as well. Any really valid exceptions, which should be kept to the minimum, must be well documented. Furthermore, the greatest possible degree of parallelism in the use of secondary headings should be maintained between different disciplines. Interdisciplinary parallelism, however, is very complex and difficult to coordinate. It may be unreasonable to expect thorough parallelism in the wide spectrum of subject analysis. Nevertheless, awareness of the advantages of parallel treatment and a conscious effort to maximize parallelism throughout the LC subject heading system will go far towards producing the ideal of complete parallelism.

NOTES

1. Lois Mai Chan. *Library of Congress Subject Headings: Principles and Application*, 2nd ed. Littleton, Colo.: Libraries Unlimited, 1986, p. 20-23. The author does an excellent job explaining "uniform headings" and "duplicate entries." The whole book, which is a detailed explication of how LC subject headings work, is outstanding.

2. *Subject Cataloging Manual*, sections H1332, H1330, H1627, and H1855.

3. Lois Mai Chan. *Library of Congress Subject Headings*, p. 182.

4. For instance, in the *Subject Cataloging Manual*, section H1855 (Manuscripts), two illustrations using six headings and two illustrations using seven headings are given.

Chapter 3

The Future

A. Subject Cataloging, the Computer, and the Future

The two most important considerations relating to subject cataloging in the future are the theoretical form of the subject heading system to be used in the next century and the increasing presence of online catalogs. Both of these factors will play major roles in the degree of success for subject retrieval in the upcoming decades. And both are closely interrelated. The computer has helped shape changes in LC's subject heading system, and LC's subject heading system has been the foundation for computerized subject access in the United States.

But the role of LC subject headings in the online environment of the future is not commonly agreed upon. Some persons, as discussed early in this treatise, feel that PRECIS or another system should replace LC.[1] This author, and others, feel that there is no substantial justification for such a substitution.[2] Other persons, almost unbelievably, feel that no formal subject retrieval system will be needed in the future because of keyword searching or similar methodologies, or at least that the form of the subject heading system will not be very vital. Although keyword searching is a helpful tool for subject access, it can only be a supplemental appendage to LC's subject heading system. In some cases keyword searching can produce faulty results. In other cases keyword searching is inadequate to access the main subject of the item because the title and other possible sources for searching do not contain the appropriate terms. And in every case, keyword searching will normally not provide access via secondary subject headings.[3]

Therefore, a formal subject system is definitely needed for the online catalog of the future. The structure and logic of the system, furthermore, will have to be at least as consistent and clearly understood in a computer environment as in a manual environment. Transfer of a faulty manual system to a computerized system will not be any kind of salvation, and in fact may even result in more confusion and retrieval difficulties. Structural and logical faults will not be corrected by or compensated for in the machine. There is no doubt that sophisticated computer programs can do many desirable things. They can make changes much more readily, they can extract and manipulate data in a number of ways, and they can search and list at a very high rate of speed. But if the data is faulty, or the conduct of the search incorrect, the data is not retrieved.

Anyone who has used systems such as OCLC and RLIN should be quite aware of this limitation. The computer can do so very much, but the data stored in the machine must be precise, logical, and well-ordered. The eyes and fingers which humans use to roam through a manual catalog are not available to the computer. In a major way, the differences between a manual system and a computer system resemble the differences between walking and using a motor vehicle. Even with bad knees, pulled muscles, and other such physical problems, a human can usually manage to get wherever he/she wants to go. But with a motor vehicle, any one of a number of problems can make the vehicle impossible or inadvisable to drive. Most of us prefer to use the greater power and speed of the vehicle, but when the machine becomes inoperable or dangerous, we have to use non-mechanical means of locomotion.

With the use of the computer as the tool for subject access, however, we do not have the option of alternative methodology. The machine (along with its operational backups) is the only choice available to us. Accordingly, the more consistent and logical the data in a computerized system is organized, the better the chances are for satisfactory retrieval.

There are other considerations which should be taken in account in a computerized subject retrieval system. First, all computer systems will not be alike or have the same degree of sophistication. Therefore, the philosophy and application of the subject access system should no more be geared to the most advanced system than an entrance to a building or room should be designed for only the most vigorous and athletic persons. If you wish to have universal access, you must have reasonable means to accomplish it. The capabilities of all types of workable computer systems should be accommodated.

With the most sophisticated systems, for example, the heading "Agriculture--Illinois--Maps" could be accessed by simply "Illinois--Maps." But a less-advanced or different type of system may not be able to access in the same manner. Therefore, adding as a second access point the gathering level "Illinois--Maps" to augment "Agriculture--Illinois--Maps" is highly desirable. The additional subject does no harm, and might even be of value in the most sophisticated computer systems. It also is in accordance with the gathering levels and secondary headings principles expounded above. Until subject cataloging systems universally make this type of secondary heading completely redundant, the practice should be retained. This example is just one illustration of why the LC subject heading system should not be modified to only the requirements of the most advanced computer systems. In fact, for an uncertain number of years into the future, the LC subject heading system will have to be serviceable to subject catalogs which are not online as well as those which are.

Second, it is vital that the entire array of subject headings assigned to any cataloging record be fully displayed, and in the order created by the cataloger. (If the computer system does not put headings in the order assigned, this deficiency should be remedied.) With the full display, the user knows all of the subjects assigned as well as their order and therefore is better informed to make judgments and choices. Without the full display, the user does not know the entire subject context nor the value/importance given to each subject as suggested by the order. (As mentioned above, it is important that the user be educated about the significance of subject heading order.)

In addition, the full display gives the exact headings with the exact sequence of the structural elements. If, for example, a person using a sophisticated system that can extract any element in LC's logical strings searches under "Education" plus "Bibliography," the full display will be very helpful in determining exactly what has been retrieved. Among others, "Education" plus "Bibliography" may retrieve the following headings:

Education--Bibliography
Education--Philosophy--Bibliography
Education--History--Bibliography

It may well make a difference to the user which of these headings applies to the record involved. Of probably greater import to the user is to have the full display indicate which subject is actually present on any given cataloging record when "Philosophy" plus "Bibliography" are the search terms and the partial result is:

Philosophy--Bibliography
Philosophy--History--Bibliography
History--Philosophy--Bibliography

or when "History" plus "Bibliography" are the search terms and the partial results is:

History--Bibliography
History--Philosophy--Bibliography
Philosophy--History-Bibliography

Similarly, it would make a big difference whether "China--Study and teaching--United States" or "United States--Study and teaching--China" is retrieved using the three elements as search terms. In the same vein, knowing the exact result of a search using "Japan," "United States," "Commercial policy," and "Politics and government" would be of considerable assistance. Among the results of such a search could be the following subject arrays:

Japan--Commercial policy
United States--Politics and government
Japan--Politics and government
United States--Commercial policy
Japan--Commercial policy
Japan--Politics and government
United States--Foreign relations--China
Canada--Commercial policy
Canada--Politics and government
United States--Foreign relations--Japan

If the computer conducted the search so that the search terms were only matched against one subject at a time, none of the four hypothetical subject arrays for the last example would occur. Since no single subject presently has that combination of four search terms, the result would be zero retrieval. But if the computer searched all subjects assigned to a cataloging record, bypassing the existence of individual headings, the four hypothetical subject arrays plus others could be the results. Or if in lieu of a formal subject search with controlled vocabulary, a keyword search using "Japan," "United States," "Commercial policy," and "Politics" was done, presuming keyword access to subjects, the retrieval would be the same. So a full display of subjects is needed no matter what type of computer system is utilized. Otherwise, the user is often not sufficiently informed or else is misinformed.

Third, the online relationship between the actual subject headings in a library's catalog and LC's voluminous subject heading listings should be clearly determined. There are two general possibilities. One is to completely separate the library's catalog from LC's subject heading listings, that is, to establish different files for each. This is the most logical and practical approach, for the two entities have decidedly contrasting purposes. After all, the library's catalog is somewhat analogous to a comprehensive encyclopedia while LC's subject heading listings are similarly loosely analogous to an unabridged dictionary. Basically, the catalog provides bibliographical information directly and access to other information indirectly. Basically, LC's subject heading listings provide lists of appropriate terminology along with guidelines for usage. The roles of the catalog and LC's subject heading listings are therefore quite dissimilar, as are the encyclopedia and dictionary. To intermix a comprehensive and complex encyclopedia and an unabridged and complex dictionary would probably create a jumble and would serve no worthwhile purpose.

Another somewhat valid analogy is the catalog as a novel or other book, and LC's subject heading listings as an unabridged dictionary. There is no good reason to integrate the book with the dictionary, for the combination would produce a very unsatisfactory volume marked by confusion and unnecessary excesses in size. Some books, for example, readers, do provide some vocabulary along with the text. But only the most basic readers provide the entire vocabulary needed. Therefore to integrate two huge and complex files with substantially opposing functions is neither theoretically sound nor practical. Just as the reader of a book can readily refer to the dictionary when necessary, the user can easily go from one file to another, presuming that the changeover is simply one command or similar uncomplicated operation.

The second option is to integrate the library's online catalog with LC's subject heading listings. In addition to the objections and difficulties elaborated above, there might be additional problems involved with the everyday use of the combined files. Unless somebody devises a clever way to avoid such problems, one or more of the following scenarios would probably occur. First, some users might not be able to clearly differentiate between the catalog and LC's subject heading listings. Similar confusion now occurs between valid headings and cross-references in the "red-books," so it could easily be presumed that at least as much confusion might result in a more complex environment. Second, if the headings, with or without subdivisions, that are actually used in the catalog are the only ones listed, it would tend to give the impression that none others are valid. Third, if all possible headings, including all possible usage of subdivisions, are listed, the file would be virtually endless.

Fourth, if the file contains LC's subject heading listings more or less as they currently exist, integrated with the library's catalog, the discrepancies between the potentialities of LC's subject heading listings and the realities of the catalog would surely evoke much confusion. In many cases, LC's subject heading listings would have no corresponding entry in the catalog. In many other cases, the heading in the catalog would have no corresponding entry in LC's subject heading listings, or the catalog heading would be longer and/or more complex than the entry in LC's subject heading listings.

Fifth, the interval between entries in LC's subject heading listings would be excessively irregular. Some headings would seldom or never be used while others might be used very frequently. Therefore the space needed to list the actual catalog entries (even in a truncated form) will vary from nothing to screen after screen after screen. Such great spatial disparities between entries in an authority listing would be a prime way to destroy the usefulness of the listing.

For a variety of reasons, the computer files containing a library's actual living catalog and LC's subject heading listings should be separately maintained. Perhaps somebody has devised or will devise a method for overcoming all of these problems in a large scale environment, but this author is not aware of any possibilities.[4] Besides, the value of such an integration can be seriously doubted, as discussed above.

B. The Form of the Library of Congress Subject Heading System in the Future

Partly because of the demands and characteristics of the computer, and partly because of other factors, the rate of change and improvement of the LC subject heading system has increased in the last decade or so. A substantial number of changes have been made to the structure/logic, terminology/semantics, and detail/specificity of LC subject headings in recent years. (A comparison of the 9th and 11th editions will show this clearly.) Many of the improvements have been minor or cosmetic. However, a number of changes which have been enacted appear to suggest the increasing presence of philosophical or theoretical principles or some sort of comprehensive plan.

It has been reported that the Subject Cataloging Division is working on the development of principles for their system.[5] This project is highly commendable. Even if all they accomplish is to put into print the philosophical bases of their current subject heading thinking and application, along with making consistent the irregularities which may contradict their principles, they will have produced a very significant work of great utility to the international library community. Throughout much of the present volume, this author has agreed with the Library of Congress in whole or in part, and has recommended putting specific realities of LC practice into print, or extending current practice to cover a broader spectrum of the system with the result also made a part of printed policy.

But as helpful as the public promulgation of LC current policy and practice would be, it is not enough. The Library of Congress should seriously consider the ideas and theories of outside persons and organizations, and in coordination with such external persons and groups, come to a consensus as to the best form for the LC subject heading system of the future. No matter how LC may feel about it, LC does not just catalog for itself but for an international community and therefore the international community should have a significant role in helping to shape the subject access of the future. And the contributions of outsiders should go a lot beyond the present relationship of LC encouraging suggestions and being more or less receptive to ideas. Persons and groups external to LC should have definite input into the overall theoretical scheme for LC subject headings, not just patchwork bits and pieces here and there. Using a streamlined, easier to use version of the *Subject Cataloging Manual* as a supplemental looseleaf volume of lists, a hardbound main volume containing general and specialized philosophical principles which have been mutually agreed upon should be developed to cover all possible subject access situations.[6]

In other words, a comprehensive all purpose theoretical code of much broader scope than the *Manual* and in a more cohesive and palatable form should be produced by the Library of Congress in collegial cooperation with outside elements.[7] This joint effort could be a committee such as that utilized to produce AACR2. Or it could be LC formally working with external advisors or consultants. In any case, the codification of the LC subject heading system should not just be an explanation of LC's current policies and practices. The new subject code should incorporate new ideas, structures, techniques, terminology, etc.

This may sound like a proposal for radical restructuring of the LC subject heading system, but it is not. Using to the fullest the principles in this volume (which were in large part derived from LC themselves and to some extent from the ideas of others), plus similar theoretical material from the international community, a moderately altered LC subject heading system which is more universally agreed upon and most importantly of greater value for subject access may well be achieved in our lifetimes.

Establishment of a cooperative comprehensive subject code by the end of this millennium is achievable,[8] and does not by any means mean the destruction of the LC system as we know it. Speaking for myself and at least some others interested in the development of a code, we have not come to bury LC, but to raise it. As has been done for descriptive cataloging by AACR2, and for personal, organizational, and geographical names by LC's online authority files, LC's subject heading system should take a few giant steps forward, be comprehensively codified, and thereby complete the trilogy of modern cataloging. With the maturation of twentieth-century cataloging thus accomplished, the threshold of the next millennium will be approached with a little more confidence and control.

C. Some Predictions for the Future

The last two essays discussed the future of Library of Congress subject headings in relation to the computer and a subject heading code. The first is already a reality and the second a real possibility. This essay goes even farther into the future and deals with even more speculative and time-distant concepts. Six predictions are given below.

1. LC subject headings will continue to be a major and effective force in the library world for at least one or two generations even if they do not accelerate their current rate of development. Because of their long history and wide influence, they will continue to exist for a while no matter how modestly LC responds to changing demands and expectations. How long LC subject headings ultimately last and the scope of their future influence will to a considerable extent depend on the degree of LC's responsiveness to public needs, including codification. (Another major factor, of course, will be the effectiveness and attractiveness of alternative systems and methods.) LC has shown in the 80's that they are capable of substantial change. The 90's may well be the crucial decision-making period in LC subject heading history, even more than the turbulent 80's. Don't be surprised if LC survives the 90's in at least as good shape as before that decade. This book would not have been written if the author had thought that there was little hope for LC.

2. LC subject headings will continue to improve in structure, terminology, and specificity. The extent of this improvement, though, is uncertain at this point, and whether the amount of adjustment will satisfy the uncertain needs of the future library commu-

nity is also cloudy. What is certain is that they must sustain their upgrading efforts.

3. LC will continue to improve the documentation for their subject heading system and its application. Even if a formal subject heading code is never officially forthcoming, LC will continue to move toward that direction by making external guides such as the *Subject Cataloging Manual* better and more useful, and by making clearer and more valuable the presentation of data in their subject heading listings. It seems quite likely that we have seen the last edition of the "red books." It is hoped, however, that LC continues to publish at least for a while an offline printed version such as they are currently issuing on microfiche. There are three reasons for retaining a printed form of LC subject headings. First, not everybody will have easy access to the online version. Second, it is always sound policy to have a backup to online systems. And third, although LC subject headings online have several good aspects, they also have some disadvantages compared to print forms. On the positive side, online headings are more up to date, the same terminal that provides topical headings also provides personal name, geographic name, and organization name data, and official headings can be instantly obtained by requesting any indexed unofficial headings (or see references). On the negative side, the online subject authority file is typically slower, does not allow the user to scan other headings in the vicinity, and sometimes is forced to present important data on second and subsequent screens thus introducing the possibility that the user may miss part of the information. Overall, though, the online subject authority file is a big step forward and a positive sign that the Library of Congress is progressing in its development.

4. More headings will be applied on cataloging records, both at the Library of Congress and by other organizations using the LC subject heading system. In part this will be because the computer will be able to accommodate an increased amount of headings so much better than catalog cards could. In part this will be because of public sentiment for more access points and thereby increased potential for retrieval.

5. LC will adopt some new techniques, concepts, or facets which will aid in the improvement of LC subject headings. Among the

possibilities are several items mentioned previously in this book, that is, new structures, more see references, better working terminology for the LC system and its application, and two levels of headings.

6. LC subject headings may possibly be the nucleus for an international multilanguage, multicultural subject heading system that is bound to develop some day. It seems as if just about everything else is becoming internationalized, so why not subject access? There are of course more problems to overcome with verbal subject access that with many other types of phenomena, but the task, this author feels, is not impossible. If LC is not a main component of such an international system, it will without doubt become isolated and wither and eventually cease to exist. It all depends on LC's flexibility and adaptability as well as its continuing overall effectiveness. LC can be the cornerstone or a millstone. Let's hope that with the cooperation of the international library community the former will be the case.

NOTES

1. For example, see Richard V. Janke, "Time for an Alternative," *Ontario Library Review* 63:200-205 (September 1979).

2. The opinions of several persons are given in William E. Studwell, "Why Not an 'AACR' for Subject Headings," *Cataloging & Classification Quarterly* 6, no. 1:3-9 (Fall 1985).

3. A good review of the problems of the online catalog, including issues relating to keyword searching are given in James R. Dwyer, "The Road to Access and the Road to Entropy," *Library Journal* 112, no. 14:131-136 (September 1, 1987).

4. A method for partially integrating the two files, but using two separate commands, is given in Noelle Van Pulis, and Lorene E. Ludy. "Subject Searching in an Online Catalog with Authority Control," *College and Research Libraries* 49, no. 6:523-533 (November 1988).

5. Response by Mary K. D. Pietris *American Libraries* 18:958 (December 1987) to article by William E. Studwell, entitled "The 1990s: Decade of Subject Access," in the same issue. Pietris states that a subject code is not needed.

6. For more details of this concept, see William E. Studwell, and Paule Rolland-Thomas. "The Form and Structure of a Subject Heading Code," p. 167-168. The authors outline some proposals as to the form a subject code might take.

7. An extended proposal for a subject code, including the opinions of others, is presented in William E. Studwell, "Why Not an 'AACR' for Subject Headings?" References to the need to comprehensively improve LC or to better docu-

ment the system and its application are scattered throughout recent literature. For example, see Mary Dykstra. *LC Subject Headings Disguised As a Thesaurus*, p. 46, and Fran Caplan. "Real People Subject Headings," letter in response to Dykstra in *Library Journal* 113, no. 11:6 (June 15, 1988). The author inquires as to why there is no simple guide to LCSH logic and arrangement.

8. See William E. Studwell, "The 1990s: Decade of Subject Access," *American Libraries* 18:958, 960 (December 1987). The author proposes that a subject code should be undertaken, and that it could be achieved in the 1990s.

Bibliography

The items not listed in the text are good background material on the subject.

Bates, Marcia J. "Rethinking Authority Control for Online Catalog Subject Access" (unpublished paper, 1988).

Berman, Sanford. *Prejudices and Antipathies: A Tract on the LC Subject Heads Concerning People*. Metuchen, N.J.: Scarecrow Press, 1971.

Berman, Sanford. "Proposed: A Subject Heading Code for Public, School and Community College Libraries," *HCL Cataloging Bulletin* 39:1-5 (March/April 1979).

Blanc-Montmayer, Martine, and Françoise Danset. *Choix de vedettes matières à l'intention des bibliothèques*. Nouv. éd. Paris: Cercle de la librairie, 1987.

Caplan, Fran. "Real People Subject Headings," letter to the editor in *Library Journal* 113, no. 11:6 (June 15, 1988).

Cataloging Service 122:16-18 (Summer 1977).

Cataloging Service Bulletin 35:37-38 (Winter 1987).

Cataloging Service Bulletin 39:27 (Fall 1987).

Cataloging Service Bulletin 39:27 (Winter 1988).

Cataloging Service Bulletin 40:46 (Spring 1988).

Cataloging Service Bulletin 41:83-84 (Summer 1988).

Chan, Lois Mai. *Library of Congress Subject Headings: Principles and Application*. 2nd ed. Littleton, Colo.: Libraries Unlimited, 1986.

Chan, Lois Mai, Phyllis A. Richmond, and Elaine Svenonius, eds. *Theory of Subject Analysis: A Sourcebook*. Littleton, Colo.: Libraries Unlimited, 1985.

Cochrane, Pauline A. *Improving LCSH for Use in Online Catalogs*. Littleton, Colo.: Libraries Unlimited, 1986.

Dale, Doris Cruger, and Betty-Ruth Wilson. "A Survey of the Literature on Subject Analysis for 1984-1985," *Library Resources & Technical Services* 30:261-289 (July/September 1986).

Dwyer, James R. "The Road to Access and the Road to Entropy," *Library Journal* 112, no. 14:131-136 (September 1, 1987).

Dykstra, Mary. "Can Subject Headings Be Saved?," *Library Journal* 113, no. 15:55-58 (September 15, 1988).

Dykstra, Mary. "LC Subject Headings Disguised As a Thesaurus," *Library Journal* 113, no. 4:42-46 (March 1, 1988).

Gorman, Michael. "Fate, Time, Occasion, Chance, and Change: or, How the Machine May Yet Save LCSH," *American Libraries* 11:557-558 (October 1980).

Haykin, David Judson. *Subject Headings: A Practical Guide*. Washington, D.C.: U.S. Government Printing Office, 1951.

Henige, David. "Library of Congress Subject Headings: Is Euthanasia the Answer?," *Cataloging & Classification Quarterly* 8, no. 1:7-19 (1987).

Hildreth, Charles. "LCSH Needs Hierarchical Restructuring," *American Libraries* 15:529 (July/August 1984).

Intner, Sheila S. "ASCR: The American Subject Cataloging Rules (Part 1)," *Technicalities* 8, no. 7:5-7 (July 1988).

Janke, Richard V. "Time for an Alternative," *Ontario Library Review* 63:200-205 (September 1979).

Library of Congress Subject Headings. 11th ed. Washington: Library of Congress, 1988.

Library of Congress Subject Headings: A Guide to Subdivision Practice. Washington: Library of Congress, 1981.

Markey, Karen, and Francis Miksa. "Subject Access Literature, 1986," *Library Resources & Technical Services*. 31:334-354 (October/December 1987).

Marshall, Joan K. *On Equal Terms: A Thesaurus for Nonsexist Indexing and Cataloging*. New York: Neal-Schuman, 1977.

McKinlay, John. "Australia, LCSH and FLASH," *Library Resources & Technical Services* 26:100-108 (April/June 1982).

Miksa, Francis. *The Subject in the Dictionary Catalog from Cutter to the Present*. Chicago: American Library Association, 1983.

OCLC Annual Report, 1987/88. Dublin, Ohio, OCLC, 1988.

The Oxford Dictionary of Quotations. 3rd ed. Oxford: Oxford University Press, 1979.

Studwell, William E. "Academic Libraries and a Subject Heading Code," *Journal of Academic Librarianship* 12:372 (January 1987).

Studwell, William E. "Codeophobia: Five Possible Reasons Why Some Persons Do Not Support a Theoretical Code for Subject Headings," *Technicalities* 9, no. 2:13-15 (February 1989).

Studwell, William E. "The 1990s: Decade of Subject Access," *American Libraries* 18:958, 960 (December 1987).

Studwell, William E. "A Structural Step Backward?," *RTSD Newsletter* 12:28-29 (Summer 1987).

Studwell, William E. "Subject Suggestions 1-7," *Cataloging & Classification Quarterly*, 8, no. 2 (1987/1988) and subsequent issues.

Studwell, William E. "Why Not an 'AACR' for Subject Headings?" *Cataloging & Classification Quarterly* 6, no. 1:3-9 (Fall 1985).

Studwell, William E., and others. "Library of Congress Period Subdivisions for . . . ," *Cataloging & Classification Quarterly*, 1982-1987 (ten articles).

Studwell, William E., and Paule Rolland-Thomas, "The Form and Structure of a Subject Heading Code," *Library Resources & Technical Services* 32:167-169 (April 1988).

Subject Cataloging Manual: Subject Headings. Rev. ed. Washington: Library of Congress, 1985.

Van Hoesen, Henry B. "Perspective in Cataloging," *Library Quarterly* 14:102-103 (April 1944).

Van Pulis, Noelle, and Lorene E. Ludy. "Subject Searching in an Online Catalog with Authority Control," *College & Research Libraries* 49, no. 6:523-533 (November 1988).

Wepsiec, Jan. "Library of Congress Subject Headings Pertaining to Society," *Cataloging & Classification Quarterly* 2, no. 3/4:1-29 (1982).

Index